BIBLIOGRAFIA
CHICANA

ETHNIC STUDIES: AN INFORMATION GUIDE SERIES

Series Editor: Curtis W. Stucki, Head, Catalog Division, University of
Washington Libraries

Other books on Ethnic Studies:

PUERTO RICANS—*Edited by Lillian Lopez***

CHINESE—*Edited by Thein Swe***

ASIANS—*Edited by Thein Swe***

**in preparation

The above series is part of the
GALE INFORMATION GUIDE LIBRARY

The Library consists of a number of separate Series of guides covering
major areas in the social sciences, humanities, and current affairs.

General Editor: Paul Wasserman, Professor and former Dean, School of
Library and Information Services, University of Maryland

BIBLIOGRAFIA CHICANA

A GUIDE TO INFORMATION SOURCES

Volume 1 in the Ethnic Studies Information Guide Series

Arnulfo D. Trejo

Professor of Library Science
University of Arizona
Tucson

Gale Research Company
Book Tower, Detroit, Michigan 48226

**Library of Congress
Cataloging in Publication Data**

Trejo, Arnulfo D
    Bibliografia chicana.

    (Ethnic studies information guide series; v. 1) (Gale information
guide library)
    Includes indexes.
    1. Mexican Americans--Bibliography. I. Title.
Z1361.M4T73   [E184.M5]   016.973'04'6872   74-11562
ISBN 0-8103-1311-1

To Annette

VITA

Arnulfo D. Trejo is by training both a librarian and educator with degrees from the University of Arizona, Universidad de las Americas, Kent State University, and the National University of Mexico. He is Professor of Library Science at the University of Arizona, Tucson, Arizona. Other books by Dr. Trejo are BIBLIOGRAFIA COMENTADA SOBRE ADMINISTRACION DE NEGOCIOS, DICCIONARIO ETIMOLOGICO DEL LEXICO DE LA DELIN-CUENCIA, and DIRECTORY OF SPANISH-SPEAKING/SPANISH SURNAMED LIBRARIANS IN THE U.S. His articles have appeared in FOLKLORE AMERICAS, UNESCO BULLETIN FOR LIBRARIANS, WILSON LIBRARY BULLE-TIN, and the ALA BULLETIN.

CONTENTS

Contents

PREFACE

Bibliographies are like compasses--indispensable for proficient navigation.
Surely researchers, educators, librarians, publishers, and book dealers can all
do better "steering" by knowing what has been written, where, when, and by
whom. It is equally important to identify the lacunae, for this too offers guidance in terms of where additional information is needed and even suggests possible format--print or nonprint? In preparing this annotated bibliography,
my objective has been to bring together titles of monographic works concerning
the Chicano life experience. Some are less relevant than others, but because
they are often cited in various compilations, I felt that it was time these works
were examined and placed in their proper perspective. Since the intent has
been to include only those works which I could personally examine, there are
titles, some of considerable value, which have escaped inclusion because it was
not possible to locate them in time to meet the established publication deadline.
My only consolation is that perhaps the titles which have been included will
lead the reader to other sources to fill whatever gaps may exist. I particularly
hope that the reader will be motivated to seek more writings by Chicano authors, for in doing so he is bound to acquire a more accurate and well-rounded
portrayal of the Chicano, together with all that makes up our fortunes and mis-
fortunes. From 1826 when Timothy Flint published the first American novel with
a "Mexican" background entitled FRANCIS BERRIAN OR THE MEXICAN PATRI-
OT until just over a decade ago, Anglo authors have been doing most of the
writing about our people. Many of these writings have contributed to the
negative image which in some cases is still held about us today.

As this bibliography deals with Chicanos, works about Mexicans have been omit-
ted. Only in special cases where the subject sheds light on the present status
of Chicanos have a few titles been selected for inclusion. Manuel Gamio's
MEXICAN IMMIGRATION TO THE UNITED STATES serves as an example.
Books on such topics as bilingualism and bicultural education have also been excluded when these topics are developed within the context of education per se.
The same applies to publications on acculturation, race relations, and migrants.
However, these same topics have been included when they are importantly related to Chicanos. Most of the titles listed would qualify for a core collection
in an academic library. A representative number of them are also suitable for
a high school library. It should be stressed, however, that inclusion of a pub-

lication in this work does not mean it is recommended for a Chicano collection. It is hoped that the collation and annotation which accompanies each entry will provide the reader with enough information to make a decision on the appropriateness of a particular work for his purposes.

A special effort has been made to represent as many subject areas as possible, giving preference to contemporary writings by Mexican American authors. The increased and continuous flow of Chicano materials, plus the numerous titles that were uncovered in the process of compiling this work, convinced me that my contribution to Chicano bibliography could best be accomplished by representing a wide range of subject areas rather than by trying for exhaustive inventories of writings in selected fields. Once this decision was made, special consideration was given to bibliographies which can be used by those persons interested in seeking additional material for further study.

Realizing the importance of serial publications to research, I have supplemented the basic text with a directory of currently published periodicals and newspapers as well as a list of those periodicals and newspapers for which no data could be obtained. In addition, the interest in Chicano materials has caused a number of new and relatively unknown publishers to spring up and undertake the printing of manuscripts which heretofore have been spurned by some of the more commonly known publishing houses. To facilitate the acquisition of these publications, a directory of the names and addresses of the publishers has been provided.

The scope in terms of time extends from 1848 to the present. The year 1848 has been chosen as the date of demarcation, for on February 2 of that year, the signing of the Treaty of Guadalupe Hidalgo granted full American citizenship to the people residing within the boundaries established by that official document. This Treaty that guaranteed freedom of religious worship, and stipulated that the Spanish language could continue to be spoken, and that customs and traditions could be practiced with no restrictions, legally recognized a new group of Americans who would be different by virtue of their historical and cultural background. So it was that the first Mexican Americans or Chicanos came into being. The history section includes a few titles that cover the Texas–Mexico conflict which eventually led to the independence of that state. This exception has been made to allow the reader to view present-day Chicanos with all of their socioeconomic and political ramifications from a broader historical background.

In the course of this work I have used the terms Chicano and Mexican American interchangeably as though they were synonymous. They are not! Any person of Mexican extraction with an American citizenship may be designated as a Mexican American. (I prefer it without the hyphen.) Not all Mexican Americans however, are Chicanos. In the words of Richard A. Garcia, "The Chicano is basically any person of Mexican ancestry who calls himself a Chicano. It provides a sense of identification not given to them by the majority of people in the United States. This word not only furnishes identity; it carries a whole philosophical meaning. A Chicano is a person who is proud of his heritage, a person who is responsible and committed to helping others of his people."[1] I prefer to use the term Chicano, but have used both to avoid redundancy. For the same reason I have occasionally used Raza and Mexicano.

Anyone who has ever compiled a bibliography cannot help but become indebted to librarians. I am no exception. In preparing this work I have received help from many librarians and library assistants. Rather than singling out names, I would like to express my gratitude and thanks to all the library staff members of the University of Arizona who so graciously gave me their assistance. I am further indebted to all those persons who provided information for the "Directory of Newspapers and Periodicals." A word of thanks also goes to the Director and office staff of my main department, the Graduate Library School for favors received while this work was in progress. Another word of appreciation is also in order for Gale Research Company for recognizing the worthiness of the subject. In the preparation of the manuscript I have been endlessly assisted by my wife, Annette. Without her help this book could not have been completed.

---

1. Richard A. Garcia, POLITICAL IDEOLOGY: A COMPARATIVE STUDY OF THREE CHICANO YOUTH ORGANIZATIONS. Master's thesis, University of Texas at El Paso, 1970.

ARRANGEMENT

The bibliographic entries are divided into five major headings: General Reference Works, Humanities, Social Sciences, History, and Applied Sciences. The entire arrangement is in keeping with the subject organization used in libraries. For example, entries in the Humanities division are alphabetically arranged under philosophy, religion, language, literature, etc. Literature, to carry the example further, is then subdivided under Bibliography, Anthologies, and Literature.

The letter-numeric system used to number individual entries is patterned after the one used by Constance M. Winchell in her GUIDE TO REFERENCE BOOKS published by the American Library Association in 1967. The system has the combined advantage of identifying each entry numerically and by subject.

The information given for each entry includes the author (when available), title and imprint (publisher, place, and date), as well as the collation (paging, whether illustrated or containing maps, tables, bibliographies, index, etc.) All entries are then followed by annotations, most of which are descriptive. Some are critical and a few are descriptive and critical. Direct quotes have been used where the work in question is highly technical and the editor has not wished to chance misconstruing the ideas of the author. Quotes have been also used for emphasis and to capture the full essence of the meaning intended by the writer. The bibliography ends with author and titles indexes and a glossary.

ABBREVIATIONS

app.	appendix	port.	portrait
aug.	augmented	pref.	preface
biblio.	bibliography	read.	reading
b & w photos.	black and white photographs	recomd.	recommended
		ref.	reference
chap.	chapter	reprod.	reproduction
col.	color		
comp.	compiler	rev.	revised
draws.	drawings	sugg.	suggested
		trans.	translated, -or
ed.	edition, editor (pl. eds.)	vol.	volume
enl.	enlarged		
facsim.	facsimile		
fnn.	footnotes		
gloss.	glossary		
l	leaves		
n.d.	no date		
no.	number		
p.	page		
pap.	paper		

INTRODUCTORY ESSAY

The urgency created by newly established ethnic studies programs and the increased demand for and interest in information relevant to the heritage of Chicanos prodded librarians into compiling bibliographies as a means of partially fulfilling these needs. Never have so many "bibliographies" been compiled with Chicanos as the subject than in the last decade. Unfortunately, many of them are the product of well-meaning aficionados who are only superficially acquainted with Chicanos and who are not versed in the art of bibliography. Ray Padilla summarizes the results in these words: "Many compilations which are labeled 'Chicano' are embarrassingly half-baked and add little or nothing to the Chicano's awareness of himself, his history, or his culture. The gabacho perspective continues to predominate."[1]

Prior to the middle sixties little or nothing was said or written about ethnic studies. The concept of specialized curriculum designed for students of a particular ethnic group was until then only an idea which remained mostly in the minds of a few farsighted individuals. By and large educators at all levels frowned upon specialized studies of this nature, considering them meaningless or just plain unnecessary. However, the pressure of over twenty-two million Afro-Americans could not be easily ignored. Reluctantly, precious new doors to knowledge began to open for them. Their success, though limited and long overdue, also encouraged Chicanos and American Indians, among other "invisible" minorities, to voice their problems and articulate the inequities which have hampered their political and socioeconomic development in America. The words "culture," "heritage," "identity," and "pride" were being heard and repeated with added vigor and confidence. As these terms reverberated from one end of the country to the other, they gained acceptance and even imparted a national awareness to members of other ethnic groups who over the years had deceived themselves into believing that they had been assimilated in the mythical "melting pot." So it was that individuals who had previously denied or given scant attention to their national origin were now busy consulting libraries in search of

---

1. Ray Padilla, "Apuntes para la documentacion de la cultura Chicana," EL GRITO 5 (Winter 1971-72): 42.

information which would enlighten them on their historical and cultural roots.

When ethnic studies finally became a reality, many librarians were caught re-hashing the cataloging code, planning computerized libraries for the year 2001, and allowing libraries to stagnate and become overgrown with interim weeds. There was money to employ librarians to catalog the books which came from the Near East and South Asia. There were librarians who could converse fluently with the dignitaries who came to our universities from Jordan, the Soviet Union, India, and Japan. But when it came to Chicano Spanish even the libraries lo-cated in the heart of the Southwest were unable to produce professional librari-ans who could establish a dialogue with the students who were asking for mate-rials to support Chicano studies programs.

During the student riots, which heralded the end of complacency in most educa-tional institutions, librarians listened--mostly from a distance. On May 1, 1968, the LIBRARY JOURNAL carried this piece of news, written with obvious pride:

> Libraries and librarians remained singularly uninvolved in the dis-turbances which followed the assassination of Martin Luther King, Jr., with vandalism almost nonexistent, even in facilities located in the hardest hit areas....[2]

There are, of course, librarians who always do their homework quietly and do it well. For example, the student problems of the sixties were skillfully anti-cipated at the library of California State University at San Francisco. Barbara Anderson has this to say:

> Months in advance (i.e., as much as six months to a year before any of the demonstrations) we were taking note of the movements toward Black Studies and Ethnic Studies. As responsive librarians, we naturally set about ordering the important books and periodicals in these fields.[3]

Libraries, with a few exceptions, have escaped being singled out as unresponsive educational institutions. This omission can be interpreted as a harsher indict-ment, for it becomes glaringly obvious that they have been of little importance in the lives of La Raza.

To pinpoint the source of libraries' "low visibility" for minorities, it is neces-sary to look at the libraries themselves. We know that they have been orga-nized mainly to serve the middle-class Anglo society. Therefore, until the last few years, it was unimportant for libraries to attract librarians who were not Anglo-Saxon, middle-class, and Protestant. Thus, when these institutions were confronted with the necessity to serve Chicanos and other minorities, head li-

---

2. "Riots Bypass the Libraries," LIBRARY JOURNAL 93 (May 1, 1968): 1843.

3. Barbara Anderson, "Ordeal at San Francisco State College," LIBRARY JOUR-NAL 95 (April 1, 1970): 1276.

brarians must have felt somewhat inadequate when they did not have the required professional staff for the assignment. Despite the fact that there are in excess of six million Mexican Americans in the Southwest, I was able to locate sixty Chicano librarians for entry in the 1973 DIRECTORY OF SPANISH-SPEAKING/ SPANISH-SURNAMED LIBRARIANS IN THE UNITED STATES. And sad to say, with a few exceptions, nearly all are in non-decision-making positions.

The blame for this situation does not lie solely with libraries. Library schools have also helped to perpetuate the social exclusiveness which has prevailed in the endemic libraries of the Southwest by training librarians for the conventional library whose policies, in some cases, date back to at least the middle of the last century. Under these circumstances it is not surprising to find Anglo libra-rians--like so many other middle-class Anglo educators who have come to the Spanish/Mexican borderlands--operating from the premise that all patrons, re-gardless of their ethnic and economic background, are equipped with the skills and knowledge needed to take advantage of this country's educational and cul-tural facilities. The lack of understanding of the differentness which exists with-in the total population of the region explains the underrepresentation of ethnic minorities in our libraries today. Here also lies the explanation as to why books, libraries, and schools are often viewed as tools of Gringolandia designed and developed to enhance its particular needs with no concern for those who do not fit the mold.

Eventually, the weight from outside forces was such that the blissful tranquility of librarians was at last shaken. Workshops and special institutes were held in various parts of the country to create an awareness for the need of libraries for Latinos. Funds were acquired from the federal government to build collections of print and nonprint materials. Outreach programs were devised and implement-ed in an effort to serve the unserved. Since librarians were now dealing with groups which they did not know, it became necessary to conduct surveys to for-mulate new library concepts and models which could possibly help to draw the potential library patron. In the beginning many of the efforts put forth met with little success. For example, the new collections that were built with the Chicano reader in mind contained a sizeable number of books from Mexico, from Spain, and from all over Spanish America. To assure that the collection had bulk, books about Cubans, Puerto Ricans, Eskimos, American Indians, and Blacks were all lumped together with the few titles by or about Mexican Ameri-cans. For the most part, these collections went unused. And no wonder! Much of what was assembled turned out to be mere junk. Without the benefit of a selection policy and a qualified staff, materials were bought indiscriminately. But, then, how could a policy be drawn without knowing the community to be served? Obviously, this was hardly possible, and the end results were meaning-less collections of books which had little in common with their intended readers.

Libraries can become the right arm of ethnic studies, but only if librarians are willing to commit themselves wholeheartedly to the cause. Librarians can, of course, continue to play the "safe" role of noninvolvement, but there is the danger that their libraries may in time lose the status they enjoy as learning centers. Their function, which is to complement and supplement the instruction imparted in the classroom, will be questioned more and more. Already there are cases where students and faculty have taken it upon themselves to bootleg "libraries" in their own departments. They justify this action by saying that libraries have not given them the kind of service they need. The bootlegged library may appear to be an answer to the immediate problem, but we know that collections of books alone do not constitute libraries. By the same token, librarians who are not responsive to the needs of their patrons and potential users are deceiving themselves if they believe that they have functional libraries.

The lack of reading materials has not really been a problem. They are available and becoming more plentiful all the time. Librarians by nature are pack rats and the bigger the budget at their disposal the more packing they manage to do. In the end, it seems that the difficulty has been the inability of librarians to bring together the potential user and the wealth of information which they have in their libraries. It is the hope of the author that the foregoing information together with the work which follows will in some measure serve to close this gap between library and user and between the Chicano and his search for identity and cultural awareness.

GENERAL REFERENCE WORKS

GENERAL REFERENCE WORKS

Guides & Indexes

AA-1 Castaneda, Carlos E., and Dabbs, Jack Autrey. GUIDE TO THE LATIN AMERICAN MANUSCRIPTS IN THE UNIVERSITY OF TEXAS LIBRARY. Cambridge: Harvard University Press, 1939. x, 217 p. Index.

> Since the guide was intended for the study of the history and culture of Latin America and the former Spanish possessions in what is now the United States, only a relatively small fraction of its entirety can be said to be relevant to Chicanos. But if the quantity is low, the quality of these rare books and manuscripts is high. All documents are alphabetically arranged by geographic area. Those which contain material for Mexican American studies are California, New Mexico, and Texas. Supplementary items can also be located under Mexico. The description of each document includes, in addition to author and title, number of leaves or pages, size, and notes the presence of illustrations and maps. In some cases a brief descriptive note accompanies the bibliographic entries.

AA-2 COMEXAZ: NEWS MONITORING SERVICE. Oakland, Calif.: Comite de Mexico y Aztlan, 1973-   . Monthly.

> The purpose of this index is to facilitate research on contemporary Chicano clippings taken from the ARIZONA REPUBLIC, DENVER POST, LOS ANGELES TIMES, SAN ANTONIO EXPRESS, EL PASO TIMES, SAN FRANCISCO CHRONICLE, and SANTA FE NEW MEXICAN, all of which are indexed by subject, byline, and geographic location. Coverage includes socioeconomic and political areas. Also included on a selective basis are clippings on sports, natural disasters, accidents, travel, social and cultural news, book reviews, advertisements, marriages, and obituaries. A cumulative annual index is announced.

3

AA-3 Cumberland, Charles C. THE UNITED STATES-MEXICAN BORDER: A SELECTIVE GUIDE TO THE LITERATURE OF THE REGION. Supplement to RURAL SOCIOLOGY 25 (June 1960). x, 236 p. Index. Pap.

A handy guide for scholars which contains a wealth of information in essay format on the socioeconomic and political conditions of the Spanish borderlands and their peoples. Coverage extends from Mexican independence to 1958. With a few exceptions, writings about the colonial period of the Southwest are omitted, as are "light readings." The guide is important because it includes pertinent literature from both sides of the border, but unfortunately most of it is by Anglo writers. Of the twelve chapters, at least the following three should be of special interest to researchers in the area of Chicano studies: (1) the Spanish-speaking population of the United States; (2) education; and (3) aspects of culture, values, religion, folklore, health, and sanitary conditions. The chapter on bibliographies and guides should also be consulted for other possible sources of information. References are made to books and monographs, government publications, theses and unpublished manuscripts, and articles in journals. Includes author index.

AA-4 Institute of Labor and Industrial Relations. University of Michigan--Wayne State University Research Division. DOCUMENT AND REFERENCE TEXT: AN INDEX TO MINORITY GROUP EMPLOYEMENT INFORMATION. Ann Arbor, Mich.: 1967. viii, 602 p. App.

A computer-generated literature index relating to employment and employment-related problems of minority workers. References to Mexican Americans are located by the use of a key-word-in-context indexing system. Entries are arranged by document number, then author. Materials published between 1956 and 1966 are included.

AA-5 Rivera, Feliciano. A GUIDE FOR THE STUDY OF THE MEXICAN AMERICAN PEOPLE IN THE UNITED STATES. San Jose, Calif.: Spartan Bookstore, 1969. xv, 226 p. Biblio. B & w photos. Draws. App. Facsims. Maps.

Using an outline form, the author traces the historical background of Mexican Americans. Complemented by a limited "basic" bibliography. Varied documents and photos included in appendix. A good substitute for this work is item DA-3.

AA-6 Saunders, Lyle. A GUIDE TO MATERIALS BEARING ON CULTURAL RELATIONS IN NEW MEXICO. Albuquerque: University of New Mexico Press, 1944. 528 p.

A selection of published and manuscript materials pertaining to cultural relations between Indians, Spanish-speaking people and Anglos in New Mexico. Dictionary-guide indexes 263 titles arranged by author with short annotations. Supplementary sections divide material into bibliographies and indexes, historical periods, and specific cultural groups. Includes author and subject indexes.

Bibliography of Bibliographies

AA-7 Clark Moreno, Joseph A. "A Bibliography of Bibliographies Relating to Studies of Mexican Americans." EL GRITO 5 (Winter 1971-72): 47-79.

The whole issue cited is devoted to the subject of Chicano bibliography, but since it is divided into two major parts and is the product of two different authors, the annotations will be written accordingly. Clark Moreno's half of the issue is primarily an unannotated listing of bibliographies concerned with Chicanos, dating to the 1800s. Included are short and long bibliographies. A few are simple handouts prepared for local library patrons, others are published in journals or parts of books, and still others are individual monographs. Not all are restricted to materials by or about Mexican Americans. A few are definite Mexican bibliographies which in some cases could be used as selection aids, depending on the orientation given to the Chicano collection. With the bibliographies cited by Padilla (see infra) and the 457 entries listed in this section, a total of 513 references are provided.

AA-8 Padilla, Ray. "Apuntes para la documentacion de la cultura Chicano." EL GRITO 5 (Winter 1971-72): 3-46.

This issue stands as a landmark because until its appearance the compilation of bibliographies on Chicanos poured forth without evaluative criticism. Padilla's provocative critique analyzes the development of Chicano bibliography from 1848 through the 1960s. He points out that during the first and second stages which lasted until 1959, the stress had been on history and the social sciences. Further, until the 1920s Anglos had been the bibliographers with Anglos as their target readers. After the 1960s, however, Chicanos themselves began preparing their own bibliographies (see item AA-9). This is the first of a two part issue. See item AA-7 for annotation on the second part.

Bibliography - General

AA-9 Barrios, Ernie, ed. BIBLIOGRAFIA DE AZTLAN: AN ANNOTATED

CHICANO BIBLIOGRAPHY. San Diego, Calif.: Centro de Estudios
Chicanos Publications, San Diego State College [University], 1971. 174
p. Index. Pap.

Journal articles and monographs arranged alphabetically
by author under such subjects as history, education,
health, literature, and sociology make up the bulk of
this work. In addition there are three separate sections
to complement the main body of material. The first
contains a few serial publications (some of which are no
longer published). Another section lists bibliographies,
and a third section lists Chicano newspapers, some of
which have ceased publication. Only the imprint is
given for monographs, leaving out the collation. One
wonders about the wide range of titles chosen to represent a bibliography that is limited to Aztlan. Uneven-
ness is also reflected in the annotations; some skillfully
state the character of the work involved, others seem
less specific. Nevertheless, they were written by specialists in most cases and their recommendations offer
guidance to those building Chicano collections. More-
over, this is where the strength of this bibliography lies,
for whether they are critical or descriptive, the annotations present a Chicano's viewpoint and call attention
to the biased nature of some authors in writing about
Chicanos.

AA-10 California. State College, Fresno. Library. AFRO- AND MEXICAN-
AMERICANA: BOOKS AND MATERIALS IN THE LIBRARY OF FRESNO
STATE COLLEGE RELATING TO THE HISTORY, CULTURE AND PROB-
LEMS OF AFRO- AND MEXICAN AMERICANS. Fresno: 1969. 109 p.

Listing of books, periodicals, government publications,
master's theses, and graduate study papers arranged by
Library of Congress classification number and author.
Entries not separated by ethnic group. Gives only author, title, and date.

AA-11 California. State College, Hayward. Library. CHICANO BIBLIOGRA-
PHY. Hayward: 1970. x, 70 p. Pap.

The title is deceiving for while works by and about Chicanos are included, most of the entries are concerned
with Mexico and its people, the Southwest (California,
in particular), Puerto Ricans, Blacks, and other subjects
such as bilingualism, minority problems, and agricultural
labor. Resources include books, periodicals, bibliographies, pamphlets, state and federal documents, and children's literature. Brief annotations are given when the
titles are not self-explanatory. The 476 entries are organized by subject areas. An author index is provided
as well as a library study guide which precedes the bib-

liography. Primarily of use to those who have access
to the library holdings listed.

AA-12 California. State University, Fullerton. Library. MEXICO AND THE
SOUTHWEST COLLECTION: A BIBLIOGRAPHY AND DIRECTORY OF
MATERIALS, SERVICES AND AGENCIES.... Alfredo H. Zuniga, coordi-
nator. Fullerton: 1974. vi, 192 p. B & w photos. Ports. Pap.

As the title indicates, this work is more than a bibliography, and perhaps therein lies its weakness as there is
marked disparity in the materials included. It appears
that the subject was not delimited sufficiently to establish boundaries of coverage. The result is a wide va-
riety of materials lumped together, and not always within context. Mexican imprints make up a large portion
of the entries. The Southwest is represented mostly by
print materials by or about Mexican Americans. Entries
are alphabetically arranged by author under subject headings. No annotations or indexes are included. The
second half contains, among other listings, periodical
articles (mostly from Chicano newspapers), audiovisuals,
publishers and distributors of Chicano materials, a few
organizations, and the Spanish-language radio and TV
stations in California. Considering this as the first product of Chicano graduate students in library science,
there is hope for more and better bibliographies concerning La Raza.

AA-13 California. University. University at Los Angeles. BIBLIOGRAPHY.
Mexican American Study Project. Advance Report, no. 3. Prepared by
the staff. Los Angeles: Division of Research, Graduate School of Business Administration, 1966. vii, 101 p.

Emphasis on the urban Chicano of the Southwest. Listing
is composed of literature of general interest (annotated
after 1940), publications on education and related subjects, rural life, and migrant labor. The last section
includes bibiliographies. Entries are listed according to
the format of the material and by period: pre-1940 and
post-1940. Format categories include books, pamphlets,
periodical articles, government publications, dissertations,
master's theses, and unpublished materials.

AA-14 California. University. University at Los Angeles. REVISED BIBLIOG-
RAPHY. Mexican American Study Project. Advance Report, no. 3.
Bibliographical essay by Ralph Guzman. Los Angeles: Division of Re-
search, Graduate School of Business Administration, 1967. 122 p. Pap.

The scope of the revised edition remains the same as
that of the first one. The differences lie in the addition
of new items and the arrangement of material. It is arranged alphabetically by author under the following major

divisions: books, journal articles, unpublished materials, and bibliographies. As there is no subject arrangement and the entries are restricted to basic bibliographic information (imprint not always complete; collations and annotations are omitted), the usefulness of this work is limited. The most unique listing is that of unpublished dissertations and theses, although no mention is made of the criteria for their selection. The introductory essay by Guzman is helpful because it provides an overview of the existing literature by and about Chicanos.

AA-15 Flynn, Barbara, et al., comps. CHICANO: A SELECTED BIBLIOGRA-PHY. San Bernardino and Riverside Counties, Calif.: Inland Library System, 1971. 93 p. Pap.

Although described as a partially annotated bibliography of English and Spanish language materials by and about Chicanos, content reveals it to be a diversified assortment of titles whose coverage varies from El Cid to the Klu Klux Klan and from pre-Columbian Mexico to the Apache frontier. The bulk of the print materials is concerned with Mexico; several titles are also Spanish imprints. Some historical background publications are cited, but the emphasis is on contemporary materials for adults, young adults, and children. Among the diverse entries are a few print and nonprint materials by and about Chicanos. Listed are books, pamphlets, periodicals, newspapers, filmstrips, slides, and records. Of special value to patrons and librarians in the San Bernardino and Riverside counties as each item is coded to indicate its location in the libraries of the Inland Library System.

AA-16 Jordan, Lois B. MEXICAN AMERICANS: RESOURCES TO BUILD CULTURAL UNDERSTANDING. Littleton, Colo.: Libraries Unlimited, 1973. 265 p. Apps. Index.

This two-part book lists with annotations selected materials considered by the compiler to be suitable for readers from junior high through college. The first part, devoted to print materials in English "related" to Chicanos, starts with the often-mentioned publications about Mexico and its people and continues with entries concerning Mexican Americans on such topics as history, education, health, art, and literature. The second part includes nonprint materials--films, recordings, maps, and transparencies. The few materials dealing with Chicanos are buried among the abundant Mexican titles. The appendices consist of biographical sketches of distinguished Mexican Americans, organizations, press associations, periodicals, and newspapers. In this section, the compiler has attempted to cover too many areas with

the result that their coverage is superficial. Outdated
information and inaccuracies are recorded as the work
is based on secondary sources. A useful reference tool,
but should be used with caution.

AA-17 Keating, Charlotte Matthews. BUILDING BRIDGES OF UNDERSTAND-
ING BETWEEN CULTURES. Tucson, Ariz.: Palo Verde Publishing Co.,
1971. 233 p. Index.

Companion to the author's BUILDING BRIDGES OF UN-
DERSTANDING, 1967. "Spanish Americans" (Chicanos
and Puerto Ricans) are included in this annotated bibliography devoted to various ethnic groups. Prepared
for parents and teachers working with children in pre-
school and primary, upper-elementary, junior high, and
high school levels. Author and title indexes.

AA-18 Loventhal, Milton, et al., comps. BIBLIOGRAFIA DE MATERIALES TO-
CANTE AL CHICANO: A BIBLIOGRAPHY OF MATERIALS RELATING
TO THE CHICANO IN THE LIBRARY, CALIFORNIA STATE UNIVERSITY,
SAN JOSE. 2nd ed. San Jose: California State University Library,
1972. viii, 222 p. Pap.

The second edition was selected for inclusion because it
lists more than 400 new entries. Includes books, theses, dissertations, a list of periodical titles, government
documents, and nonprint materials. Pamphlets are omitted. To facilitate the use of the material, call numbers
are included. A close look at the print material titles
reveals that many have little or no relevance to the Chicano; not all books about Mexico and Indians are neces-
sarily pertinent to the American of Mexican descent.
Usefulness is further limited by arrangement of the material and lack of complete bibliographic information. With
the exception of periodicals, the various types of materials are listed alphabetically under subject headings
such as agricultural labor, bilingualism, Cesar Chavez,
Indians of Mexico, Mexican Americans, Mexico, Mexico City, Southwest, etc. Since no collations are provided the researcher is left in doubt as to the usability
and applicability of the items cited. A one-page supplement lists films relevant to La Raza.

AA-19 Marin, Christine N., comp. A GENERAL BIBLIOGRAPHY AND GUIDE
TO MEXICAN-AMERICAN MATERIALS IN THE CHICANO STUDIES COL-
LECTION AND IN THE HAYDEN LIBRARY, ARIZONA STATE UNIVER-
SITY. Tempe: Chicano Studies Library Project, Hayden Library, Arizo-
na State University, 1973. 66 p. Pap.

A straight alphabetical listing by author's name of those
print materials (several Mexican imprints included) selec-

ted to complement and supplement the Chicano Studies
Program. The emphasis is on books, but also includes
a few government publications and nonpublished materials such as theses. No annotations, but includes call
numbers.

AA-20 Najera, Carlos, comp. CHICANOS: A SELECTIVE GUIDE TO MATE-
RIALS IN THE UCSB LIBRARY. Santa Barbara: University Library, University of California at Santa Barbara, 1971. iv, 78 p. Indexes. Pap.

Reflects the range of the library collection on the life
and culture of Chicanos. Lists books, curriculum development guides, and government publications. The
fact that the guide is neatly published, has entries alphabetically arranged by author under a broader range
of subject headings, and includes call numbers and author and subject indexes makes this bibliography useful
to both UCSB library patrons and others interested in
identifying these specialized holdings which generally
represent an adherence to a more discriminating selection
policy for a Chicano collection.

AA-21 Nogales, Luis G., ed. THE MEXICAN AMERICAN: A SELECTED AND
ANNOTATED BIBLIOGRAPHY. Stanford, Calif.: Stanford University,
Center for Latin American Studies, 1971. 162 p. Indexes. Pap.

This is a revised and enlarged edition of the 1969 bibliography. Contains 444 entries, 274 of which are annotated, and covers books, journals, dissertations, and
government documents. Emphasis on the social sciences.
Provides subject and field indexes with cross-listing of
entries.

AA-22 Ortego, Philip D., comp. SELECTIVE MEXICAN-AMERICAN BIBLIOG-
RAPHY. El Paso, Tex.: Border Regional Library Association in coopera-
tion with the Chicano Research Institute, 1972. x, 121 p. Pap.

By listing books, periodical articles, reports, documents,
and some unpublished materials such as dissertations and
mimeographed publications, the compiler has attempted
to show "the varied literary interests of Mexican Americans and their forebears who settled in the American
Southwest." Much material is brought to light, but
omission of pertinent bibliographic data and the inclusion
of items without annotations and without regard to format, as well as their entry under a wide assortment of
subjects which differ in scope, diminishes the usefulness
of the work.

AA-23 PROYECTO LEER BULLETIN. Washington, D.C.: Organization of American States, 1968 - . Quarterly

Designed to provide information on library materials useful to the Spanish-speaking in the United States. Many
entries included are pertinent to Chicanos. Titles are
arranged under broad subject categories and evaluated
according to reading levels: easy (grades k-3), inter-
mediate (4-6), advanced (7-10), and more advanced
(11-12). Includes print and nonprint materials accompanied by brief annotations. The addresses of distributors and publishers are also given.

AA-24 Quintana, Helena, comp. A CURRENT BIBLIOGRAPHY ON CHICANOS,
1960-1973, SELECTED AND ANNOTATED. Albuquerque: Zimmerman
Library, University of New Mexico, 1974. 47 p. Index. Pap.

One of the better-compiled inventories of current writings by or about Chicanos. Most titles are for educated
adults, but also included are representative selections
for children and young adults. Teachers will be pleased
to find textbooks listed. Titles are arranged alphabetically by author and the reading level is designated for
each entry. There is an index which divides works by
grade level and designates professional monographs, but
a subject and title index are lacking. Annotations vary
from none to a well-formulated descriptive or sometimes
critical statement. A list of current Chicano periodicals
and a directory of Chicano publishers are included.

AA-25 Revelle, Keith, comp. ¡CHICANO! A SELECTED BIBLIOGRAPHY OF
MATERIALS BY AND ABOUT MEXICO AND MEXICAN AMERICANS.
Oakland, Calif.: Latin American Library of Oakland Public Library,
1969. 21 p. Pap.

Limited in scope, but could prove useful in organizing
a basic Chicano collection. This briefly annotated bibliography of books, periodicals, articles, reports, and
speeches is alphabetically arranged by author under the
type of material. Includes prices. The work is dated;
most items listed can now be found in more comprehensive and up-to-date bibliographies.

AA-26 Schramko, Linda Fowler. CHICANO BIBLIOGRAPHY: SELECTED MATE-
RIALS ON AMERICANS OF MEXICAN DESCENT. Bibliographic Series,
no. 1. Rev. ed. Sacramento, Calif.: Sacramento State College Library, 1970. 124 p. Index. Pap.

Contains 1,000 items including periodical articles, master's theses, doctoral dissertations, and ERIC microfiche.
Divided into broad categories with a detailed subject index and cross references.

AA-27 Stanford University. Center for Latin American Studies. THE MEXICAN

AMERICAN: A SELECTED AND ANNOTATED BIBLIOGRAPHY. Stanford, Calif.: 1969. 139 p. Index. Pap.

Contains 274 critical annotations of selected books and articles focusing mainly upon contemporary issues. Arranged alphabetically by author with subject index to numbered annotations.

AA-28 U.S. Cabinet Committee on Opportunity for the Spanish Speaking. THE SPANISH-SPEAKING IN THE UNITED STATES: A GUIDE TO MATERIALS. Washington, D.C.: Government Printing Office, 1971. 175 p. Pap.

The Spanish-speaking in this case are Cubans, Mexican Americans, and Puerto Ricans. This work is an expanded revision of the 1969 original edition published by the governmental agency known as the Inter-Agency Committee on Mexican American Affairs. Lists books, periodical articles, government publications, theses, newspapers, journals, audiovisual material, Spanish-language radio and television stations. Some entries accompanied by brief annotations. Contains a subject index to books and periodicals.

AA-29 Utah. University. Marriott Library. CHICANO BIBLIOGRAPHY. Bibliographic Series, vol. 1. Salt Lake City: 1973. 297 p.

This work comprises several unannotated lists of print and nonprint materials available at University of Utah libraries. The volume is arranged in seven sections with entries in alphabetical order. No subject indexes or cross references. Useful sections on government documents, selections from Education Resources Information Center (ERIC), and periodical articles. Unfortunately, the compilers do not indicate what journals were researched or the periods covered. Seemingly the emphasis is on recent articles listed in standard bibliographic sources.

Librarianship & Library Resources

AB-1 California. Los Angeles State College [University]. A LIBRARY GUIDE TO MEXICAN-AMERICAN STUDIES. Los Angeles: John F. Kennedy Memorial Library, 1969. 14 p. Pap.

Contains information on how to conduct research relating to Chicanos with brief information on sources such as bibliographies, abstracts, indexes, government publications, and reference books. Also has a list of subject headings which could lead to pertinent print materials reflected in the card catalog. A second part includes titles of bibliographies, general surveys, indexes, and abstracts, as well as a few master's theses and projects. A useful publication which, hopefully by now, has been revised, updated, and made more useful as a source of information.

AB-2 Dudley, Mariam Sue. CHICANO LIBRARY PROGRAM. UCLA Library Occasional Papers, no. 17. Los Angeles: University of California Library, 1970. 85 p. B & w photos. Pap.

Describes with written text and illustrations a one-quarter, no-credit course that was devised to provide one hundred high-potential Chicano students with library skills. By performing the sixteen "tasks" at their own pace, the students are instructed in the use of the college library. A useful guide which could be even more effective if additional sample forms reflected names and book titles of particular interest to Chicanos.

AB-3 Eshelman, William R., ed. WILSON LIBRARY BULLETIN 44 (March 1970): 681-800.

William Ramirez, the guest editor, has synthesized the content of this issue with these words: "Each of the contributors...in his own way seems to suggest that the basic intellectual needs of the Spanish-speaking person in the United States boils down to four: equal educational opportunity, realization by the Anglo that the Latino's culture is as good as his own, information and resources, and cultural reinforcement" (714). Articles in the issue are concerned with Puerto Ricans, Cubans, and Chicanos, in particular. Among the Chicano contributors are Robert P. Haro, Ysidro Ramon Macias, Armando Rodriguez, and Arnulfo D. Trejo.

AB-4 Polan, Morris, ed. CALIFORNIA LIBRARIAN 34 (January 1973): 3-63.

John L. Ayala, guest editor, introduces this issue by stating, "We hope to let you know about what has been done, what is being done, and what needs to be done to improve Chicano library service. Our purpose is to help you learn and maybe eventually, obtain your aid in improving Raza library service at all levels" (5). Topics vary from the writings of the pre-Columbian cultures of Mexico to Chicanos in children's literature and the different outreach programs that have been designed specifically to serve La Raza. Joe Salazar, the only contributor not from California, writes about how the Chicano community is being served by the Denver Public Library. Other contributors include Josue Aranda, Daniel Duran, Nelly Fernandez, Robert P. Haro, Julia

M. Orozco, Elizabeth Martinez Smith, and Jose Taylor.

AB-5 U.S. Department of Health, Education and Welfare. Office of Education. Bureau of Libraries and Educational Technology. A SYSTEMS ANALYSIS OF SOUTHWESTERN SPANISH-SPEAKING USERS AND NON-USERS OF LIBRARY AND INFORMATION SERVICES DEVELOPING CRITERIA TO DESIGN AN OPTIMAL LIBRARY MODEL CONCEPT. FINAL REPORT. Washington, D.C.: National Education Resources Institute, 1972. Varied Paging. Apps. Graphs. Tables. Pap.

> Through a survey of library users and nonusers, and libraries at various levels from elementary and parochial schools to junior college and institutional libraries, as well as librarians and persons in city government, this report draws a profile of Chicano library users and potential users. On the basis of an analysis of data collected from eleven cities in the states of Arizona, California, Colorado, New Mexico, and Texas, model library concepts were developed as possible means of improving library services to Mexican Americans. The report offers three basic recommendations: (1) training to successfully implement outreach programs, (2) changes which can be effected without significant budget modification, and (3) innovations in management and library methodologies which give acceptance to successful bilingual programs. A reprinted student's library guide designed for Chicanos is included as part of the appendices.

AB-6 Vadala, Julia, ed. HISPANO LIBRARY SERVICES FOR ARIZONA, COLORADO, AND NEW MEXICO: A WORKSHOP HELD IN SANTA FE, NEW MEXICO, APRIL 30, MAY 1-2, 1970. Boulder, Colo.: Western Interstate Commission for Higher Education, 1970. v, 45 p. B & w photos. Pap.

> Papers were presented with these objectives in mind: (1) to furnish an overview of Mexican Americans in the states mentioned above, (2) to explore opportunities for new library programs to reach the unserved, and (3) to plan strategies for implementation of library plans at the local level. The three main Chicano speakers included Horacio Ulibarri (Historical and Cultural Perspectives), Cecilio Orozco (Language and Bilingual Education Perspective), and Manuel Carrillo (Human Relations and the Library).

Directories

AC-1 DIRECTORIO CHICANO. Hayward, Calif.: Southwest Network, 1973. 16 p. Pap.

> Includes the name and address of schools which have

definite Chicano-oriented educational programs, publishers and book jobbers, as well as a partial listing of newspapers and magazines--active and defunct. The information is organized under four broad geographic regions, West Coast, Southwest, Midwest, and East Coast, and also by state. Only those states with a fairly large Chicano population are listed.

AC-2 INTER REGIONAL MIGRANT SERVICES DIRECTORY (REGION V & REGION VI). Austin, Tex.: Migrant Referral Project, 1974. 100 p. Pap.

A listing of human services available to migrants in Arkansas, Illinois, Indiana, Louisiana, Michigan, Minnesota, New Mexico, Ohio, Oklahoma, Texas, and Wisconsin. The entries are grouped under four general categories: education, employment, health, and social services. The various services are then arranged alphabetically by state and city, listing address and telephone number. The directory was compiled in the hope that it would be "useful to every human service provided referring and/or directing their migrant clients to existing services in another region or state." To facilitate its use by Chicanos, Spanish is used when appropriate.

AC-3 Trejo, Arnulfo D., ed. DIRECTORY OF SPANISH-SPEAKING/SPANISH-SURNAMED LIBRARIANS IN THE UNITED STATES. 2nd rev. and aug. ed. Graduate Library School Monograph, no. 4. Tucson: Bureau of School Services, College of Education, University of Arizona, 1973. 21 p. Pap.

As the title suggests, the directory is not limited to Chicano librarians, but since it is the only reference tool of its kind, it can be used to identify the few who are in the profession. The alphabetically arranged entries include name, business and home addresses, ethnic group, area of specialization, and fluency in Spanish.

AC-4 U.S. Cabinet Committee on Opportunity for the Spanish Speaking. DIRECTORY OF SPANISH ORGANIZATIONS IN THE UNITED STATES. Washington, D.C.: Government Printing Office, 1971. x, 231 p. Indexes. Pap.

This directory contains data on 207 groups, not all of which are concerned with Chicanos. Six major organizations, three of which have a Chicano membership, are listed first. Included is basic information such as name, address, telephone, principal officer, scope, date founded, ethnic membership, frequency of meetings, objectives, and availability of literature about the organization. The same information is furnished for sub-

sequent groups which are listed alphabetically by state,
city, and name of organization. One index lists groups
by name, another by subject. Though dated, it can be
a useful source of information for individuals and agencies wishing to identify nonprofit organizations of Spanish-
speaking peoples.

Biography

AD-1 Morin, Raul. AMONG THE VALIANT: MEXICAN AMERICANS IN WW
II AND KOREA. Los Angeles: Borden Publishing Co., 1962. 290 p.
B & w photos.

In addition to the personal narratives of Chicanos who
distinguished themselves in WW II and the Korean War,
the work includes historical background on Mexican
Americans and the part played by members of this ethnic
group in all battle fronts and all branches of the armed
forces.

AD-2 Newlon, Clarke. FAMOUS MEXICAN AMERICANS. Foreword by Dr.
Uvaldo H. Palomares. New York: Dodd, Mead & Co., 1972. 187 p.
Index. Ports.

Nineteen biographies written in easy, readable style
make this book particularly appropriate for young adults.
Representing a cross-section of contemporary Chicanos,
the author has identified personalities in sports, politics,
and education, and leaders such as Cesar Chavez, Rodolfo Gonzales, Reies Lopez Tijerina, Jose Gutierrez, and
Dolores Huerta. Among the better-known personalities
included are Lee Trevino, Anthony Quinn, Ricardo
Montalban, Trini Lopez, Vikki Carr, and Pancho Gonzalez.

AD-3 Palacios, Arturo, ed. THE MEXICAN AMERICAN DIRECTORY. Washington, D.C.: Executive Systems Corp., 1969/70 - . 224 p.

First volume of biographical listing of members of Mexican American community with "expertise in the area of
Mexican Americans" for the use of private industry and
government agencies. Entries include such information
as occupation, education, military service, employment
history, memberships, awards and honors, and published
works.

Language Dictionaries

AE-1 Trejo, Amulfo D. DICCIONARIO ETIMOLOGICO LATINO-AMERICANO

DEL LEXICO DE LA DELINCUENCIA. Manuales UTEHA, no. 365/Doble
- 12 Linguistica. Mexico, D.F.: Union Tipografica Editorial Hispano
Americana, 1968. 226 p. Biblio. Index.

> While the dictionary includes primarily Mexican and
> Peruvian argot, it does include a few pachuquismos and
> other terms used in Chicano Spanish, some of which
> have their origin in fifteenth-century Spanish. Baisa,
> bote, and jura serve as examples.

HUMANITIES

HUMANITIES

Philosophy

BA-1 Carranza, Eliu. PENSAMIENTOS ON LOS CHICANOS: A CULTURAL
REVOLUTION. Berkeley, Calif.: California Book Co., 1969. 29 1.
Biblio. Footnotes. Illus. Pap.

> A collection of thought-provoking essays in which the
> author deals philosophically with topics such as Chi-
> canos, the social movement of La Raza, values, heri-
> tage, and traditions.

Religion

BB-1 Darley, Alex M. THE PASSIONISTS OF THE SOUTHWEST, OR THE
HOLY BROTHERHOOD. 1893. Reprint. Glorieta, N. Mex.: Rio
Grande Press, 1968. viii, 119 p. Apps. Biblio. B & w draw. and
photos.

> In the introduction, Robert B. McCoy, president of the
> press which published this reprint, questions the authority
> of Darley's work. He suggests that the author's view-
> points are biased and bigoted, but "...they are histo-
> ric." With this in mind the reader is invited to read
> the first full account of the penitente brotherhood as
> recorded by a Protestant minister of the time thought to
> be self-ordained. A more objective viewpoint is pre-
> sented in Appendix I in the form of a speech delivered
> in 1965 by McCoy. Many of the photos included in
> Appendix II were taken by Charles Lummis. Appendix
> III includes a bibliography on the penitentes.

BB-2 Henderson, Alice Corbin. BROTHERS OF LIGHT: THE PENITENTES OF
THE SOUTHWEST. Illus. by William Penhallow Henderson. 1937. Reprint. Chicago: Rio Grande Press, 1962. 126 p. B & w draw. Refs.

> An informative, detailed, and well-written account of

21

the penitente brotherhood of New Mexico. The author
considers the penitentes a "folk-survival" of religious
customs which can be traced to the Third Order of St.
Francis. The surviving twentieth-century rituals and
mysticism are effectively linked to their historical background. One third of the book is devoted to translations of alabados from a penitente copy book.

BB-3 Rael, Juan B. THE NEW MEXICAN ALABADO, WITH TRANSCRIPTION
OF MUSIC BY ELEANOR HAGUE. Stanford University Publications.
University Series. Language and Literature, no. 3, vol. IX. Stanford,
Calif.: Stanford University Press, 1951. 154 p. Gloss. Pap.

From his collection of more than two hundred religious
hymns, the author has selected eighty-nine for this work
on the basis of their intrinsic value and popularity. The
alabados were collected from the region encompassed by
the San Luis Valley in Colorado and the Taos and Rio
Grande Valleys in northern New Mexico. The musical
scores which supplement the text were transcribed from
the author's recordings of the melodies sung by six native
penitentes. The translation of four hymns acquaints the
English reader with the general content of the alabados.

BB-4 Tate, Bill. THE PENITENTES OF THE SANGRE DE CRISTO: AN AMERI-
CAN TRAGEDY. 2nd ed. Truchas, N. Mex.: Tate Gallery, 1967.
53 p. Biblio. Fnn. B & w draws.

For the hermanos penitentes of New Mexico there is
self-flagellation, particularly during Holy Week. But
on Easter Sunday there is joy, for they share the resur-
rection with Christ. The author relates information
about their art and music, their sorrows and tragedies,
in describing how members of this religious order completely enwrap themselves in their beliefs and rituals.

BB-5 Weigle, Marta. THE PENITENTES OF THE SOUTHWEST. Etchings by
Eli Levin. Santa Fe, N. Mex.: Ancient City Press, 1970. 46 p.
Biblio. B & w photos. Map. Pap.

Intended as an introduction to the beliefs, practices, organization, and history of the penitente brotherhood of
northern New Mexico and southern Colorado. The work
is well-written and based on research of published and
unpublished sources.

Language

BC-1 Barker, George C. PACHUCO: AN AMERICAN-SPANISH ARGOT AND
ITS SOCIAL FUNCTIONS IN TUCSON, ARIZONA. Social Science Bul-

letin, no. 18. Tucson: University of Arizona Press, 1950. 38 p. Biblio. Gloss. Pap.

In this brief introduction to the Pachuco argot spoken in Tucson, the author studies its origin, syntax, and usage. The study is complemented by a conversation using this jargon and several Pachuco songs, some of which were composed by Lalo Guerrero.

BC-2 Espinosa, Aurelio M. ESTUDIOS SOBRE EL ESPANOL DE NUEVO MEJICO: PARTE I. FONETICA. Biblioteca de dialectologia hispanoamericana, tomo I. Traduccion, reelaboracion y notas de Angel Rosenblat. Buenos Aires: Instituto de Filologia, Facultad de Filosofia y Letras de la Universidad de Buenos Aires, 1930. 472 p. Apps. Biblio. Maps.

The focus of this scholarly study is on the Spanish spoken in northern New Mexico and in the San Luis Valley of southern Colorado. The phonetic analysis deals mostly with changes in accentuation, vowels, and consonants. One chapter is devoted to proper names. Phonetic transcriptions of texts are also included. The author's research demonstrates that the historical roots of New Mexican Spanish are directly linked to the sixteenth-century Spanish brought by the conquistadores from Castile, Andalucia, and Estremadura. A later wave of colonizers included individuals from northern Spain, e.g., Galicia and Catalonia. Nine appendices written by Amado Alonso on the problems of Spanish American dialectology complement this volume.

BC-3 _____. ESTUDIOS SOBRE EL ESPANOL DE NUEVO MEJICO: PARTE II. MORFOLOGIA. Biblioteca de dialectologia hispanoamericana, tomo II. Traduccion, reelaboracion y notas de Angel Rosenblat. Buenos Aires: Instituto de Filologia, Facultad de Filosofia y Letras de la Universidad de Buenos Aires, 1946. 409 p. Biblio. Word index.

This is the most comprehensive and in-depth study that has ever been done of the Spanish spoken in New Mexico. It explains and documents patterns of word formation. Dr. Espinosa observes that the morphology of New Mexican Spanish is basically that of Castilian Spanish and therefore needs to be researched in the Spanish spoken in the sixteenth century. But this is more than a regional study, for, as Dr. Rosenblat explains, in researching historical word antecedents and explaining linguistic phenomena, the study acquires a dimension of Spanish in general.

BC-4 Kercheville, Francis M., comp. "A Preliminary Glossary of New Mexican Spanish, Together with Some Semantic and Philogical Facts of the Spanish Spoken in Chilili, New Mexico, by George E. McSpadden." UNIVERSITY OF NEW MEXICO BULLETIN, Language Series, vol. 5, no. 3 (July 15, 1934). Albuquerque: University of New Mexico, 1934. 102 p. Biblio.

The first part consists of a glossary (with English translation) which was compiled by selecting words and phrases from printed sources and conversations not entered in dictionaries of standard Spanish. The usage of this vocabulary is not limited to New Mexico. Some of it is used in other parts of the Southwest, Spanish America, and even Spain. In section two, the author has documented the slow change which has taken place in the Spanish spoken in Chilili and throughout New Mexico. Semantic changes which have occurred in certain words are included with the author's findings, together with notes on phonology and morphology.

BC-5 Lucero Trujillo, Marcela. CHICANO SPANISH: ESSAYS ON CHICANO SPANISH. Denver, Colo.: El Valle Publications, 1973. 13 p. Biblio. Pap.
The author convincingly demonstrates that Chicano Spanish is not an inferior tongue. The language, which has been subject to environmental influences, has evolved as a form of identification for the people who speak it. Preservation of regional Spanish is encouraged to retain the Chicano's cultural heritage and to facilitate communication in standard Spanish with the entire Spanish-speaking world.

BC-6 Post, Anita C. SOUTHERN ARIZONA SPANISH PHONOLOGY. Humanities Bulletin, no. 1. Tucson: University of Arizona, 1934. vi, 57 p. Biblio. Pap.

This study, originally part of a Ph.D. dissertation, is concerned with the Spanish spoken in northern Sonora and southern Arizona. It is the language first introduced into this area by the Spanish colonists and soldiers of the sixteenth and seventeenth centuries. The Arizona material selected from oral tradition is mainly from Yuma and Tucson. Through the use of phonetic transcription, the author reflects changes in accentuation and also records the pronunciation of vowels and consonants. Various examples are used. The closing chapter includes the phonetic text of five brief tales related to the author.

Literature

Bibliography

BD-1 Dobie, James Frank. GUIDE TO LIFE AND LITERATURE OF THE SOUTH-

WEST. Dallas, Tex.: Southern Methodist University Press, 1952. 222
p. Biblio. Illus. Index.

Bibliographic guide to books on folklore, history, Mexican life, explorations, and historical fiction, giving
some brief descriptions. Index to authors and titles.

BD-2 Rojas, Guillermo. TOWARD A CHICANO/RAZA BIBLIOGRAPHY: DRA-
MA, PROSE, POETRY. EL GRITO Book Series, book 2. Berkeley, Calif.: Quinto Sol Publications, 1973. 85 p.

An unannotated bibliography covering the years 1965-72
and listing the literature falling into the above-mention-
ed categories. Most of the citations have been drawn
from Chicano newspapers and magazines, and to a lesser degree from monographs. Analytical entries are also
included for Quinto Sol publications and a few selected
monographs. Entries are alphabetically arranged under
each of the categories. Since there is no index and
the listing cites references without regard to the format
of the source, its use is not especially easy. Nonetheless, since the writings are not generally indexed in the
standard bibliographical sources, this work can prove
useful despite its limitations.

Biography

BD-3 Acosta, Oscar Zeta. THE AUTOBIOGRAPHY OF A BROWN BUFFALO.
San Francisco: Straight Arrow Books, 1972. 199 p. Distributed by
Quick Fox, Inc., 33 West 60th Street, New York 10017.

An outpouring of his inner conflicts by a Chicano from
San Francisco veiling himself as a discontented lawyer
with ulcers and anxieties, he concludes his search for
identity by admitting that since he is neither a "Mexican" nor an "American", neither Catholic nor Protestant,
he needs a new identity. He chooses to be identified
as a brown buffalo. Why buffalo? The author finds
that he has no roots in the Mexican past, but from this
ancestry he gets his brown complexion. And, weren't
the buffalo slaughtered and used by everyone, and "still
they mean no harm." Writing in a style that is clear-
cut, informal, and at times witty, the author welds this
account together effectively by making use of the raw
material of experience.

BD-4 Galarza, Ernesto. BARRIO BOY. Notre Dame: University of Notre
Dame Press, 1971. xi, 275 p.

A vivid autobiography which describes a particular way
of life common to many who migrated from Mexico during

the 1910 Revolution to various parts of the United States
and in particular the Southwest. The story begins in
the village of Jalcocotan (not far from Tepic) where the
author was born and terminates when as a teenager he
is about to enter high school in his adopted hometown
of Sacramento. In a skillfully developed style and well-
chosen language, he captures the historical and political
happenings in Mexico that led to his being brought to
the United States. The latter part of the book describes
what it's like to grow up in a California barrio. Despite his experience with acculturation, Galarza never
lost his self-image or pride in his culture.

BD-5   Garcia, Andrew. TOUGH TRIP THROUGH PARADISE, 1878-1879. Edited by Bennett H. Stein. New York: Ballantine Books, 1967. 383
p. B & w photos. Maps. Pap.

The recollections of a Texas Mexican who, after leaving
the army at the age of twenty-three, went to live
among the Indians in the wilderness of Montana. This
unique record differs from the usual Anglo accounts
about Indians, traders, and trappers. It is told with
sympathy and understanding for the Amerind and reveals
insights which come only from personal experience.

BD-6   Jaramillo, Cleofas M. ROMANCE OF A LITTLE VILLAGE GIRL. San
Antonio, Tex.: The Naylor Co., 1955. x, 200 p. B & w photos.
Ports.

A sequel to SHADOWS OF THE PAST. The author sheds
further light on the way of life as lived by the ricos of
New Mexico. She traces her ancestry back to the re-
conquest of New Mexico under Vargas in 1692, but her
story begins in 1846 with the arrival of Kearney in Santa
Fe. In reminiscing about her early years, the author
acquaints the reader with customs and traditions that
were part of a simple life in which religion played an
important role. As an adult she enjoyed love and hap-
piness until the loss of her husband. She suffered another severe blow when her daughter died violently.
As a finale, Cleo tells about revisiting Arroyo Hondo,
the "dear village" banked by the Taos Mountains, which
brings back fond memories of yesteryears. Includes
material from SHADOWS OF THE PAST (see CE-3).

Anthologies

BD-7   Castaneda Shular, Antonia, et al., eds. LITERATURA CHICANA: TEX-
TO Y CONTEXTO. Englewood Cliffs, N.J.: Prentice-Hall, Inc.,
1972. 395 p.

The editors have set out to place Chicano literature in context with that of other peoples with whom Chicanos share a linguistic, cultural, and historical heritage. The bulk of the literature is from Hispanic America with particular emphasis on Mexico and with selections from pre-Hispanic America and Puerto Rico. While there are binding ties with other Spanish-speaking peoples in the hemisphere, the differences are greater than the similarities and Chicanos may question the appropriateness of the hodgepodge of writings which have been brought together under what turns out to be a deceptive title. A portion of the selections are in Spanish with English translations.

BD-8 Huerta, Jorge A., ed. EL TEATRO DE LA ESPERANZA: AN ANTHOLOGY OF CHICANO DRAMA. Goleta, Calif.: El Teatro de la Esperanza, Inc., 1973. ii, 125 p. B & w photos. Pap.

The actos (one-act plays) included are mostly the product of students at Santa Barbara's University of California who helped form El Teatro in 1971. These plays are fashioned along the lines of those written by Luis Valdez, creator of the Teatro Campesino, except that the topics are oriented towards the urban Chicano. Some of the actos still need reworking, as the writers themselves have admitted, but regardless of their shortcomings, they were all written for the purpose of educating el pueblo Chicano in regard to social change. Notes on producing the plays are provided as well as some poetry and biographical information on the playwrights.

BD-9 Ludwig, Edward W., and Santibanez, James, eds. THE CHICANOS: MEXICAN AMERICAN VOICES. Baltimore: Penguin Books, 1971. ix, 286 p. Biblio.

This collection of selected writings consists of reprinted articles, short stories, essays, an excerpt from a novel, some poetry, and Tijerina's prison letters. As a whole they represent a panoramic picture of the Chicano experience with emphasis on contemporary issues. The diversity in views is achieved by the contributors chosen. The majority are Mexican Americans and include such individuals as Joan Baez, Eliu Carranza, Cesar Chavez, Amado Muro, Philip D. Ortego, Feliciano Rivera, Luis Valdez, and Richard Vasquez.

BD-10 Ortego, Philip D. WE ARE CHICANOS: AN ANTHOLOGY OF MEXICAN-AMERICAN LITERATURE. New York: Washington Square Press, 1973. 351 p. Biblio. B & w photos. Span./Eng. Gloss. Pap.

Intended as a textbook, this work contains folklore, poetry, drama, fiction, and expository writing. The

selections and arrangement of the book are adequate.
Its prime limitation is paucity of material in some categories, e.g., one play and a short excerpt from a novel.

BD-11 Paredes, Americo, and Paredes, Raymund. MEXICAN-AMERICAN AU-
THORS. Boston: Houghton Mifflin Co., 1972. 152 p. Gloss. of
Spanish words & phrases. Map. Ports. Pap.

Since Americo Paredes is a noted folklorist, this anthology offers creditable samples of Mexican American folklore. The short story genre is also featured along with
some poetry. Questions for discussion purposes follow
each of the selections. The chosen readings and overall arrangement of the material suggest this work as a
possible complementary text for Chicano literature, particularly at the high school and junior college level.
In addition to Paredes, other contributors are Jovita
Gonzalez, Josephina Niggli, Amado Muro, Mario Suarez, Arnulfo D. Trejo, and Nick Vaca.

BD-12 Romano-V., Octavio Ignacio, and Rios C., Herminio, eds. EL ESPEJO
-- THE MIRROR: SELECTED CHICANO LITERATURE. 5th rev. ed.
Berkeley, Calif.: Quinto Sol Publications, 1972. 280 p. Pap.

This anthology, composed exclusively of Chicano writers,
brings together short stories, poems, a full-length play,
and an assortment of unclassified bits of literature. Although this revised version includes excerpts from two
prize-winning novels, it still does not come up to the
literary level attained by the first edition (now out of
print) published in 1969. Nevertheless, this work continues to be one of the better collections of Chicano
literature. A few selections are published both in
English and Spanish.

BD-13 Salinas, Luis Omar, and Faderman, Lillian. FROM THE BARRIO: A
CHICANO ANTHOLOGY. San Francisco: Canfield Press, 1973. vi,
154 p. Pap.

Offers a glimpse of the barrio and its people through essays, poetry, short stories, a bit of folklore, and selected chapters from POCHO and CHICANO, two popular Chicano novels. The scope and usefulness of the
work is limited. Contains little material not previously
published.

BD-14 Simmen, Edward, ed. THE CHICANO: FROM CARICATURE TO SELF-
PORTRAIT. Introduction by editor. New York: New American Library, 1971. 332 p. Biblio. Gloss. Pap.

A collection of short stories effectively organized to

show how this genre was used to portray people of Mexican extraction from 1869 to the present time. Not knowing their subject, the early Anglo writers created caricatures instead of real characters. Progressively, plots and characters became more plausible, although writers such as Paul Horgan, John Steinbeck, and Ray Bradbury still narrated stories which lacked authenticity. The real world of the Chicano did not come to light in the short story until after WW II when a few Chicano authors finally began to write fiction.

BD-15 Valdez, Luis, and Steiner, Stan, eds. AZTLAN: AN ANTHOLOGY OF MEXICAN AMERICAN LITERATURE. New York: Alfred A. Knopf, 1972. xii, 410 p.

A collection of writings that range from pre-Columbian literature of Mexico to present-day emergence of cultural and political Chicano awareness. Contains essays, poetry, legends, tales, plays, ballads, selection of memoirs, and articles. There is relatively little Chicano creative literature, but regardless of the type of writing included, it all generally reflects the resistance of Chicanos to the pressures of acculturation.

Literature

BD-16 Anaya, Rodolfo A. BLESS ME, ULTIMA. Berkeley, Calif.: Quinto Sol Publications, 1972. ix, 248 p. B & w draw.

Through the eyes of Antonio Marez y Luna, a six-year-old boy, Anaya weaves a sensitive story of his own New Mexican people, their traditions, customs, and legends. The underlying conflict between reality and idealism involves Antonio's development and is presented through his consciousness, his subconscious, and interaction with other characters. Among the many customs and beliefs spawned by the union of Spaniard and Indian is one that says that the natural and supernatural shall live in harmony. Thus Ultima, the wise old medicine woman, cures ills with herbs and evil curses with "magical" powers. Such is Ultima's strength that even the terrible Tenorio fails in his treacherous deeds. Anaya's skill and eloquence as a writer lie in his ability to construct a regional story in the fashion of "costumbrismo" where local color is combined with realistic elements and the characters are used to reflect a way of life.

BD-17 Atencio, Tomas, et al., eds. ENTRE VERDE Y SECO. Introduction by Tomas Atencio. Art by Alberto Baros. Photos by Estevan Arellano and Vicente Martinez. Dixon, N. Mex.: La Academia de la Nueva

Raza, 1972. 119 p. B & w photos and draw. Gloss. Pap.

The editors have collected a sampling of the literature created by the Spanish-speaking people of New Mexico. Included are tales, anecdotes, incidents, riddles, ballads, and poetry. Together they interpret human life with its ups and downs. Almost all of the writing appears in New Mexican Spanish.

BD-18 Barrio, Raymond. THE PLUM PLUM PICKERS. Sunnyvale, Calif.: Ventura Press, 1969. 202 p. Pap.

The author has chosen the fertile area near Santa Clara, California, which once belonged to Mexico, as the setting for his social protest novel. It describes the deplorable conditions under which the migrant workers earn their living and the frustration, anger, and self-doubt they suffer. There is no marked plot; the story consists of different incidents and psychological events as they pertain to the inner and outer worlds of the characters. Recommended to readers with no previous knowledge of the plight of migrant farmworkers.

BD-19 Brito, Aristeo. FOMENTO LITERARIO: CUENTOS I POEMAS. Translated by Jose Lerma. Drawings by Al Romo. Washington, D.C.: Congreso Nacional de Asuntos Colegiales, 1974. 63 p. B & w draws. Pap.

The author, who grew up in Presidio, Texas, and who comes from an extended lineage of Tejanos, uses lucid Spanish to describe in both verse and prose characters and experiences drawn mostly from his early years when he worked in the fields. The suppressed fears, anxieties, and insecurities of the oppressed Chicanos are uniquely expressed with imagination and emotional power. Unfortunately, the full symbolical meaning of this literature will be apparent only to the most perceptive readers. The translation is well done, considering the difficulty of the material.

BD-20 Camerena, Emanuel J. PANCHO: THE STRUGGLES OF A WETBACK IN AMERICA. New York: Exposition Press, 1958. 78 p.

A novelette which gives some insights into the troubles experienced by Mexicans who cross the border illegally in search of a better life in the United States. The style is prosaic and the characters and plot are poorly developed. Suggested for those who are unfamiliar with the subject.

BD-21 Chandler, David. HUELGA! A NOVEL. New York: Simon and Schuster, 1970. 284 p.

As the title suggests, the central idea deals with the
Delano farmworkers' strike of the 1960s. The fictional
account takes place in Verde Valley, California, and
the main character, Daniel Garcia, is patterned after
Cesar Chavez. Chandler writes sympathetically about
the huelga and its supporters, but he uses the two main
characters primarily to carry the reader through a seemingly unconnected series of episodes, resorting to sell-
tactics such as sex scenes and the use of fantasy for
producing thrills. The novel, then, falls short in creating believable circumstances to illustrate aspects of human life and behavior.

BD-22 Chavez, Angelico. FROM AN ALTAR SCREEN. EL RETABLO: TALES
FROM NEW MEXICO. Illustrated by Peter Hurd. New York: Farrar,
Straus and Cudahy, 1957. 119 p. B & w draws.

According to the author, "...this is less a collection of
short stories than a running series of accounts about different generations in the same general locale." In effect, they are narratives that lack dramatic plot, but
which relate details, not of important personages but
rather of real or imaginary events and incidents pertinent to ordinary persons.

BD-23 Cox, William. CHICANO CRUZ. New York: Bantam Books, 1972.
216 p. Pap.

A two-hundred pound, tough, Texas-born coach with
lots of savvy about baseball and people, though not too
well educated, puts together the best infield in the
Pennjersey league with young, agile, and ambitious ball
players who are headed for the majors. The main characters include a Black, full of pride, hate, and deter-
mination, an Anglo, middle-class kid who rebels against
his bigoted father, a millionaire's son who is trying to
succeed on his own merits, and a Chicano who takes
pride in his heritage. Some suspense and interest is
created through subplots or incidents related to the main
characters. As a former semi-pro baseball player, the
author writes knowledgeably and clearly about the game,
but fails to delineate real characters or to record life
accurately.

BD-24 Delgado, Abelardo B. CHICANO: TWENTY-FIVE PIECES OF A CHI-
CANO MIND. Drawings by Ernesto Palomino. Santa Barbara, Calif.:
La Causa Publications, 1970? 36 p. B & w draws.

The poet's main concern is to narrate the experiences
of the people of the barrios. Because of his intense

desire to tell rather than make the reader feel, the
thoughts are direct and the elements of poetry such as
melody, rhythm, and imagery play only a minor role.
Some of the poems are in English, others in Spanish,
and some are a mixture of both.

BD-25 Delgado, Abelardo B., et al. POEMAS Y REFLECCIONES DE CUATRO
CHICANOS.... Denver: Barrio Publications, 1972? 55 p. B & w
photos.

In this small book of barrio poetry one outstanding element common to all four poets is the prevailing tone
of anger. One also hears cries of despair, sorrow,
revenge, and scorn. Occasionally feelings of love and
tenderness are expressed when the subject is mother or
sweetheart. There are few expressions of beauty or
jubilation. An excerpt from the work of each poet
follows:

. . . .
watch me...how sadly i smile,
what a tragically joyous living is my style.

Abelardo, "Frontier"

. . . .
You speak harsh, soldiers march.
I am here to kill you.
The slow death in the United States
has begun.

Reymundo "Tigre" Perez, "What Have
You Done?"

. . . .
DESMADRE   DESMADRE   DESMADRE
LET SOCIETY BE DAMNED
AND HUMANITY BE SALVAGED...

Ricardo Sanchez, "L. A. P. D."

democracy where have you hidden
you...democracy you have deserted us
where is your sister justice who
speaks so much and does so little
I tell you she's a whore
taking those who pay the best.

Juan Valdez, "Democracy Your Sister's
A Whore"

BD-26 Elizondo, Sergio. PERROS Y ANTIPERROS: UNA EPICA CHICANA.
Translated by Gustavo Segada. Berkeley, Calif.: Quinto Sol Publications, 1972. 75 p. Pap.

32

Elizondo, a native of Sinaloa, Mexico, received his
elementary and secondary education in Mexico and later
did his undergraduate and graduate studies in this country
where he now lives. His poetry differs little from the
writings of other Mexican American protest authors. He
fully engulfs the feelings, attitudes, beliefs, and awareness of Chicanismo. Thought, tone, and imagery predominate in his poems.

BD-27 Gilbert, Fabiola [Cabeza de Baca]. WE FED THEM CACTUS. Draws.
by Dorothy L. Peters. Albuquerque: University of New Mexico Press,
1954. 186 p.

These are stories told to the author when she was ten
years old. They tell about rodeos, mustangs, and the
buffalo hunt, and describe the often difficult way of
life of the Hispanos on the New Mexican llano, the
staked plains. The book is based on historical fact.

BD-28 Gonzales, Rodolfo. I AM JOAQUIN: YO SOY JOAQUIN: AN EPIC
POEM WITH A CHRONOLOGY OF PEOPLE AND EVENTS IN MEXICAN
AND MEXICAN AMERICAN HISTORY. Text in Spanish and English.
New York: Bantam Books, 1972. 122 p. B & w photos.

The name Joaquin is borrowed from the legendary folk
hero, Joaquin Murrieta. The poet uses the name sym-
bolically to represent the Chicano in the course of history. By effectively combining thought with imagery,
Gonzales has written one of the most significant pieces
of creative Chicano poetry.

BD-29 Griffith, Beatrice Winston. AMERICAN ME. Boston: Houghton Mifflin,
1948. x, 341 p. Illus. Gloss.

A narrative that combines fiction and nonfiction to
bring out the ugly and oftentimes lamentable facts concerned with the socioeconomic conditions of Mexican
Americans. Covers the zoot-suit riots of 1943.

BD-30 Hinojosa-S., Rolando R. ESTAMPAS DEL VALLE Y OTRAS OBRAS.
SKETCHES OF THE VALLEY AND OTHER WORKS. Berkeley, Calif.:
Quinto Sol Publications, 1973. 183 p. Pap.

The best way to describe this prize-winning book (written in English and Spanish) is to call it a gallery of
people and landscapes. Not important people or impressive sites, but humble individuals and seemingly unimportant things. What gives life to the subjects is the
author's mastery of a vast vocabulary and his skill in
using it to express the inner feelings of his characters
and capture the very essence of a sketch or situation

in a short story. Together these portrayals realistically
present a slice of Chicano life. Although the translation
is done quite well, the full flavor of this work will be
enjoyed by those who can read the Spanish version.

BD-31 Kirack, Alex [Gallo]. SPACE FLUTES AND BARRIO PATHS. Illustrated
by Mario Acevedo Torero. San Diego, Calif.: Centro de Estudios Chicanos Publications, 1972. 72 p. B & w draws. Gloss.

The poet, an ex-con from San Quentin, takes the reader
on a mental pilgrimage through the horrors of the barrio
and the sufferings of its people. The prevailing tone
is somber; imagery is often used and though difficult to
understand at times it can be felt. The poems are written in free verse, but their staccato beat lends them a
rhythm which seemingly spreads throughout. What melody there is does not seem pleasant to the ear. Yet it
is fitting, for the poet's thoughts are with tecatos, street-
walkers, winos, brujas, and

> Chicanos forced to give up their identity
> forever held in bondage by the whip
> and the holy cross, that enslaves
> tribes and nations

"Trail of Tears"

BD-32 Mendez-M., Miguel. PEREGRINOS DE AZTLAN. LITERATURA CHI-
CANA (NOVELA). Tucson, Ariz.: Editorial Peregrinos, 1974. 210 p.

If there is a protagonist in this novel, it would have to
be Loreto Maldonado, the poor, unkempt Yaqui who
makes a living by washing cars in a Sonoran border city
that goes unnamed. Since there is no central plot, this
character serves as the spin-off for and the connecting
link between the series of short stories, character sketches,
anecdotes, and incidents which together describe the
Mexicano way of life on both sides of the border. In
giving a faithful treatment to the poor and the rich, the
writer depicts raw reality with all its crudeness and un-
adulterated truths. He gives credence and authenticity
to characters, setting, and imagined experiences, particularly through his versatile use of the language. He
switches from standard Spanish to Chicano Spanish and
Pachuco argot, depending on the situation. The insights
into the conditions which have spawned and nurtured the
migrants of the Southwest leave the reader with a better
understanding of our neighbors to the south and the Chicano's pursuit of a better tomorrow.

BD-33 Olvera, Joe. VOCES DE LA GENTE. Perspectiva, numero I. Illustrated by Carlos Olvera. El Paso, Tex.: Mictla Publications, 1972. 40

p. B & w draws. Pap.

Neither the short stories nor the poetry can be cited for
their literary qualities. Yet the prose and verse--
whether it be with love or hate--express what it has
meant to the author to have been raised in poverty in
one of the barrios of El Paso.

BD-34 Pillsbury, Dorothy L. ROOTS IN ADOBE. Illustrated by Sam Smith.
Albuquerque: University of New Mexico Press, 1959. 232 p.

This work is about the Hispanos of Santa Fe as described
in a series of articles which for the most part originally
appeared in the CHRISTIAN SCIENCE MONITOR from
1952 to 1957. Most of the vignettes are interesting,
but the writer's style is condescending and her use of
Spanish is artificial.

BD-35 Rechy, John. CITY OF NIGHT. New York: Grove Press, 1963. 380
p. Pap.

In this moralistic novel the Texas-born Chicano writer
depicts the underworld of the homosexual lock, stock,
and barrel. The story begins in El Paso where the main
character grew up in a stunted, uncertain environment.
Finding no direction at home, he eventually escaped to
plunge himself into the big-city male prostitution scene.
Rechy gives an almost detached picture of homosexuality
and raises many questions, but provides no answers.
The author's almost journalistic style lends itself well to
descriptions of the harsh, nasty world of cities at night.
Yet it is this same style which contributes to a series
of characterizations which show little imagination.

BD-36 _____. NUMBERS. New York: Grove Press, 1967. 256 p.

Rechy's readable style, which at times suggests a touch
of Camus, has depicted homosexuals out for sex with no
strings attached, people out for sex with people they
see as "numbers," not as individuals. It is the sordid
story of the homosexual-in-the-street which gives short
shrift to the lifestyles of the many others who are homosexuals.

BD-37 Rivera, Tomas. "...Y NO SE LO TRAGO LA TIERRA" ["...AND THE
EARTH DID NOT PART"]. Translated by Herminio Rios C., in collabo-
ration with author, with assistance of Octavio I. Romano-V. Printed in
Spanish and English. Berkeley, Calif.: Quinto Sol Publications, 1971.
177 p. Pap.

This novel is a series of short stories, tales, anecdotes,
and seemingly unrelated incidents. Not until the last

chapter does it become apparent how the preceeding
narratives and characters fit into the total scheme.
However, it is this structural organization which gives
originality to the work. Various themes are of concern
to the author, but the one which stands out in this
beautifully narrated Chicano experience is that of the
individual having a measure of control over his destiny
without having to rely on the will of God.

BD-38 Robinson, Cecil. WITH THE EARS OF STRANGERS: THE MEXICAN IN
AMERICAN LITERATURE. Drawings by H. Beaumont Williams. Tucson:
University of Arizona Press, 1963. ix, 338 p. Biblio.

A study which documents for the first time how Anglo
writers of the early nineteenth century to the 1930s
inaccurately portrayed the "Mexican" of the Spanish
borderlands in literature. "Mexican" characters were
stereotyped as dull, dirty, lazy, cowardly, treacherous,
and cruel to animals and liable to steal anything not
nailed down. The explanation offered is that some
authors had never seen a Mexicano. But whether they
had or not made little difference. Their descriptions
were a reflection of prejudices which they and many
Anglo frontiersmen had brought with them to the Southwest from the South. The racist attitudes they had held
against Blacks were merely transferred to other peoples
who did not conform with Anglo-American characteristics.

BD-39 Rodriguez, Armando Rafael, comp. & ed. THE GYPSY WAGON. UN
SANCOCHO DE CUENTOS SOBRE LA EXPERIENCIA CHICANA. Crea-
tive Series, no. 2. Los Angeles: Aztlan Publications, University of
California, 1974. iii, 89 p. Pap.

With the exception of a story by veteran Chicano writer,
Mario Suarez, these stories are mostly the produce of
young Chicanos who frequently gathered around the Gypsy
Wagon at the University of California campus for rap
sessions. The writings do not always fully develop the
elements of the short story, but on the whole they depict
believable settings, characters, and situations which
illustrate an awareness and knowledge of Chicano life.

BD-40 Salas, Floyd. TATTO THE WICKED CROSS. New York: Grove Press,
1967. 361 p.

The story takes place in the early forties inside the
Golden Gate Institute of Industry and Reform. The
theme depicts the plight of racial minorities which pop-
ulate these institutions. At age fifteen Aaron D'Aragon
enters the world of prison life which for him becomes

a constant struggle for survival. The major portion of
the story deals with Aaron's fight for self-preservation
by practicing the prison code which his environment
forces him to learn. The last scene finds him waiting
to be transferred to San Quentin on three counts of
murder. The language is tough and a few Pachuco
words have been appropriately used in dialogues. On
the whole, the novel is convincing enough to show
that "rehabilitating" institutions only reinforce anti-
social thought and action through their deficiencies.

BD-41 Salinas, Luis Omar. CRAZY GYPSY. Illustrated by Tony Perales and
John Sierra. Photos. by Alexander Castro. Origenes Publication. Fres-
no: Universidad de Aztlan (California State University), 1970. 87 p.
B & w photos and draws. Pap.

Through the use of psychedelic imagery and selected
words (Spanish at times) which set the tone, the author's
lyric poetry depicts worlds where love, death, and hate
vie for dominance. While the minstrel poeticizes the
Chicano first, his free verse transcends political borders
as a voice of social protest which goes in search of
human values.

BD-42 Sanchez, Ricardo. CANTO Y GRITO MI LIBERACION (Y LLORO MIS
DESMADRAZGOS...). Illustrated by Manuel Gregorio Acosta. El Paso,
Tex.: Mictla Publications, 1970. N.p. Col. plates & draws.

As the title suggests, the author, who describes himself
as a poetic mutation, playwright, journalist, pachuco,
ex-con, and a high school pushout, gives free rein to
his inner feelings both in prose and poetry. In verse
he best captures the raw realities of Chicanismo whether
it be life in the prison or the barrio. He writes in Chicano Spanish or combines it with English and calo.

BD-43 Smith, C.W. THIN MEN OF HADDAM. New York: Grossman Publishers, 1973. 327 p.

The story takes place in the mid-sixties and evolves
around Raphael Mendez, a young Mexican American
who has been made foreman at a Texas ranch. Despite
his being raised and educated by his Anglo employers
he does not lose his cultural identity. Thus Mendez is
torn between the world in which he lives and that of
poor Chicanos of which his cousin Manuelo is a part.
He dreams of a cooperative ranch as a means to help
his people, but finds that he as well as the disadvantaged are still at the mercy of the Anglo. The novel
includes a well-structured plot with an element of suspense and a surprise ending. The characters are many-

sided and generally believable. The style does not
always lend itself to easy reading for it is rich in sym-
bolism and leans rather heavily on flashbacks. The
setting is used effectively to emphasize the peculiarities
of the region, but the use of Spanish proves more of a
detriment than an asset. Nonetheless, Chicanos have
come a long way in Anglo fiction--from caricature to
plausible and lifelike people.

BD-44 Ulibarri, Sabine R. AL CIELO SE SUBE A PIE. Madrid: Ediciones Al-
faguara, 1966. 65 p. Pap.

The themes of love and idealized woman that prevail in
this book of lyric poetry are generally universal. What
singles out the work of this New Mexican author is his
poetic language. The erudite poet has chosen the best
of his native Spanish language not solely to describe
"facts" but also as an interconnecting vehicle with which
he creates rhythm, melody, tone, and imagery.

BD-45 _____. TIERRA AMARILLA: CUENTOS DE NUEVO MEXICO. Bilingual ed. Translated by Thelma Campbell Nason. Illustrated by Kercheville. Albuquerque: University of New Mexico Press, 1971. x, 167
p. B & w draws.

Five beautifully narrated tales and a six-chapter novella
accurately depict the customs and traditions of the people in a small Mexican American village in northern
New Mexico. The author, a native of the region,
talks with simplicity and sensitivity about his early years.

BD-46 _____, ed. LA FRAGUA SIN FUEGO (NO FIRE FOR THE FORGE).
STORIES AND POEMS IN NEW MEXICAN SPANISH. Translated by
Flora V. Orozco, et al. With introduction and a story by Sabine R.
Ulibarri. Cerrillos, N. Mex.: San Marcos Press, 1971. 66 p. Pap.

The title takes its name from the short story by Professor
Ulibarri which depicts the straitlaced New Mexican customs and traditions of generations gone by. The literature that follows is the product of his students. They
may not yet have the refined techniques of the maestro,
but the value of their work lies in the perception of
life by a younger generation. The importance of the
book is that Hispanos are writing about Hispanos.

BD-47 Urista, Alberto Baltazar [Alurista]. FLORICANTO EN AZTLAN. Creative Series, no. 1. Los Angeles: Aztlan Publications, University of
California, 1971. 100 p. Pap.

One of the best lyric poets to surface in the course of
the Movimiento. The one hundred poems contained in

this work exemplify Alurista's unique style of blending
English and Spanish. In content he skillfully captures
the historical background of the Chicano as well as the
present-day struggle for socioeconomic justice.

BD-48 _____. NATIONCHILD PLUMAROJA. Illustrated by Esteban Villa and
Armando Nunez. San Diego, Calif.: Toltecas en Aztlan, Centro Cultural de la Raza, 1972. N.p.

This pocket-sized book is replete with lyrical verses of
a poet who seeks socioeconomic and political liberation
for the Chicano people. Stress is on a spiritual unity
among the "Red People with a Red Culture." Style and
techniques are those characteristic of Alurista. The language used is a mixture of English and Spanish, the Az-
tec symbols are a means of dealing with abstraction,
and free association of imagery rather than logical se-
quence all combine to make this poetry of interest to
a select rather than a general audience. Nonetheless,
the depth of his poetry springs forth from every page,
which, unfortunately, is difficult to read because of
the size of the print and the color of the paper.

BD-49 Urista, Alberto Baltazar [Alurista], and Gonzalez, Jorge, eds. EL OM-
BLIGO DE AZTLAN. San Diego, Calif.: Centre de Estudios Chicanos
Publications, San Diego State College, 1971. 92 p. B & w draws.
Pap.

With the exception of the contributions by Alurista and
Gomez, the poems in this booklet are the product of
students from the Chicano creative writing classes of-
fered by the Chicano Studies Department. The titles
of the four sections into which the work is divided give
an indication of the themes and tone of the poetry:
"The Proud Roots of Our Birth," "The Angry Clash of
Our Struggle and the Cancerous Apathy of Our Times,"
"The Joyous Liberation of Our Destinies," and "Raza,
Raza."

BD-50 Vasquez, Richard. CHICANO. Garden City, N.Y.: Doubleday &
Co., 1970. 376 p.

While the novel begins in northern Mexico around the
turn of the century, the first part is mainly concerned
with the efforts of the Sandoval family to establish itself in the United States. The second part of the story
narrates the tragic romance of Mariana, a fourth-genera-
tion Sandoval, and David Stiver, an Anglo sociology
student, who values social status and education more
than the life of his beloved. The geographical setting
is East Los Angeles, but the psychological setting is a

battleground where Chicanos struggle with acculturation
while clinging to their heritage. The author skillfully
interweaves the multivaried, socioeconomic problems
confronted by Chicanos into an informative, readable
and entertaining social-protest novel. Intended primarily for Anglos who are unaware or uninformed on these
matters.

BD-51 Villarreal, Jose Antonio. THE FIFTH HORSEMAN. Garden City,
N.Y.: Doubleday & Co., 1974. 398 p.

In this historical novel of the Mexican Revolution,
Heraclio Ines, the protagonist, was the fifth and last
child in a family of cowhands who lived on a small
hacienda in the State of Zacatecas. Heraclio is seventeen when the Revolution strikes Mexico. His valor
and horsemanship make him a natural for the dorados,
an elite cavalry corps of General Francisco Villa, in
which he later becomes an officer. The Revolution,
however, does not solve Heraclio's problems. Deep-
rooted traditions and beliefs based on ancestry and upper and lower class differences remain unconquerable
obstacles in fulfilling his love for the daughter of a
Spanish patron. In developing the plot, the author
effectively describes the troubles and sufferings of the
Mexican nation and its people. The significance of
this novel is that for the first time a Chicano writer
is interpreting the Mexican Revolution. Like Mariano
Azuela, Villarreal takes the position that the struggle,
bloody and violent as it was, and its ideals offered a
step forward, but also condemns its excesses.

BD-52 _____. POCHO. Introduction by Ramon E. Ruiz. Garden City,
N.Y.: Doubleday, Anchor Books, 1959. xii, 187 p. Pap.

The author traces the life of Juan Rubio and his son,
Richard, the main character, through various phases of
their lives. Richard was born in California and grew
up in Santa Clara. He emerges both as an individual
and a symbol of the "pocho," the first generation Mexican American who is in search of an identity within two
distinct cultures. The traumatic experiences of acculturation destroy the Rubio family. In the end, Richard
joins the Navy to fight in WW II, and perhaps finds
answers to his dilemma.

BD-53 Villasenor, Edmund. MACHO. New York: Bantam Books, 1973. 245
p. Pap.

A village in the State of Michoacan--where people
are still bound by the customs, rules, and beliefs of
Mexican tradition--serves as the opening setting for

this novel narrated by a Chicano author. The protagonist, seventeen-year-old Roberto Garcia, is persuaded
to leave his family and rural way of life to become a
Norteno, one who takes as many gringo dollars as he
can. The theme deals primarily with the troubles suffered both in Mexico and the United States by men who
enter this country as illegal farm workers. The climax
finds the hero back in his village involved in a Western-
type shootout. The novel falls in the category of escape fiction rather than interpretive literature. Except
for short commentaries that read like editorials and
which are used to introduce each chapter, the level
of technical accomplishment is comparatively modest.
Nonetheless, the story is packed with action and should
prove entertaining especially for those interested in
reading about Mexicans and Chicanos.

Fine Arts

BE-1 Dickey, Roland F. NEW MEXICO VILLAGE ARTS. Drawings by Lloyd
Lozes Goff. Albuquerque: University of New Mexico Press, 1949.
xii, 266 p. Biblio. Draws. in b & w & color. Gloss. Index.

Understanding life in the Spanish villages of New Mexico permits the author to relate how the ordinary people
use their hands creatively to provide for their physical
needs and at the same time satisfy their esthetic senses.
He writes about building a house with sunbaked adobes,
the furniture that goes inside it, tools and techniques,
and textile arts, as well as the artists who carve or
paint santos, bultos, retablos and angelitos. A portion
of the book is also concerned with Christian arts and
churches which are the joint product of Hispanos and the
indigenous people of the region.

BE-2 Espinosa, Jose E. SAINTS IN THE VALLEYS: CHRISTIAN SACRED IM-
AGES IN THE HISTORY, LIFE AND FOLK ART OF SPANISH NEW
MEXICO. Foreword by Fray Angelico Chavez, O.F.M. Albuquerque:
University of New Mexico Press, 1960. 122 p. Apps. Biblio. B &
w plates. Index. Map.

Provides a scholarly, historical account of the religious
folk art which developed in New Mexico and the San
Luis Valley of northern Colorado from about 1775 to
1900. The history portion is followed by a brief note
on each of the forty-six plates contained in this work.
Information is also provided on the three major classifi-
cations of images, i.e., retablos, bultos, and paintings
on animal skins in tempera. Further, the craft of painting and carving the sacred images is described. Ap-

propriately, the last chapter is devoted to the role played by the saints and their images in the lives of the
Hispanos. Several appendices give such information as
the distribution of the various santos in existence.

BE-3   Mills, George. THE PEOPLE OF THE SAINTS. Colorado Springs,
        Colo.: Taylor Museum, n.d. 103 p. Col. plates.

        Believing that the study of a people's art is one of the
        best ways to understand that people, the author answers
        the question, "Who are the Spanish-Americans?" Al-
        though this is not an in-depth study and is based pri-
        marily on secondary sources, the reader will find his
        interest provoked by such topics as the penitentes, the
        various church and secular rituals, and the santos. The
        narrative closes with a series of brief notes on the
        thirty-two illustrated santos.

BE-4   Quirarte, Jacinto. MEXICAN AMERICAN ARTISTS. The John Fielding
        and Lois Lasater Maher Series, no. 2. Austin: University of Texas
        Press, 1973. 174 p. Biblio. B & w and col. plates. Index. Map.

        The author discusses the dichotomy of universality and
        ethnic identity facing the Mexican American artist to-
        day. In several dialogues with such artists as Esteban
        Villa, Mel Casas, Emilio Aguirre, Rudy Trevino, and
        Ralph Ortiz, he explores what it means to be a Chi-
        cano artist and the influence of training and cultural
        background on their work. He finds that some of them
        are consciously creating art which defines their ethni-
        city while others take an individualistic approach. Yet,
        there seems to be among the artists a growing awareness
        of their ancestral heritage. The book is divided into
        two parts: (1) A brief historical survey with emphasis
        on southwestern art and architecture that have served
        as antecedents for Chicano artists with a chapter de-
        voted to the Mexican muralists Orozco, Siqueiros, Ri-
        vera, and Tamayo; (2) the work of Chicano artists from
        New York to California starting from 1901. The book
        is amply illustrated with examples of the various artists'
        works.

BE-5   Shalkop, Robert L. WOODEN SAINTS: THE SANTOS OF NEW MEXI-
        CO. Colorado Springs, Colo.: Taylor Museum, 1967. 63 p. Col.
        plates.

        The narrative part, or first half of the book, is brief
        and lacks in documentation. Yet the author gives evi-
        dence of having read widely on the subject and the
        people of New Mexico. The value of this work, how-
        ever, particularly for artists, lies in the second half.

Sixteen colored plates of <u>santos</u> from various parts of
the state are described in accompanying paragraphs which
provide, among other details, dimensions, place of
origin, biographical data on the saint, and the painter.
The quality paper on which these colored plates are re-
produced enhances the beauty of the images.

SOCIAL SCIENCES

SOCIAL SCIENCES

Bibliography

CA-1 Navarro, Eliseo G. ANNOTATED BIBLIOGRAPHY OF MATERIALS ON THE MEXICAN AMERICAN. Austin: Graduate School of Social Work, University of Texas, 1969. 53 p. Pap.

> Critically annotated listing of 134 books, articles, monographs, proceedings, reports, and audiovisual aids available in the field of social science and related disciplines. Coded by letters to indicate area of social work curriculum. See also CB-7.

General Surveys

CA-2 Burma, John H., comp. MEXICAN AMERICANS IN THE UNITED STATES: A READER. Cambridge, Mass.: Schenkman Publishing Co., distributed by Canfield Press, 1970. 505 p. Biblio.

> Essays and studies by both Anglo and Mexican American authors provide an overall view of Mexican Americans by treating such topics as prejudice, civil rights, education, employment, family, social and political behavior, health, acculturation, and assimilation. Authors include attorneys, anthropologists, historians, sociologists, educators, journalists, and others writing in their areas of expertise.

CA-3 Cabrera, Y[sidro] Arturo. EMERGING FACES: THE MEXICAN AMERICANS. Dubuque, Iowa: Wm. C. Brown Co. Publishers, 1971. ix, 99 p. Apps. Biblio. Index. Gloss. Pap.

> The author has selected such topics as education, housing, religion, cultural identity, and the treatment of Mexican Americans in literature. Although not all Chicanos will share his views, the reader is exposed to the thinking on these issues by a Mexican American

scholar.

CA-4 De Leon, Nephtali. CHICANOS: OUR BACKGROUND AND OUR PRIDE. Illustrated by author. Lubbock, Tex.: Trucha Publications, 1972. 93 p. Biblio. B & w draws. Photos. Pap.

There are documented sources where more profound and comprehensive information can be found on Chicanos, but this booklet has special merit because the writing emanates from the heart and displays deep feelings which come from bearing long years of social injustice. Its focus is on the conditions of La Raza in Lubbock, Texas.

CA-5 Duran, Livie Isauro, and Bernard, H. Russell, eds. INTRODUCTION TO CHICANO STUDIES: A READER. New York: Macmillan, 1973. v, 585 p. Biblio. Gloss. Graphs. Maps. Tables. Pap.

Selected readings of reprinted material, organized into three parts--yesterday, today, and tomorrow--make up the main body of this work. The writings of Jose Vasconcelos, Octavio Paz, and Armando B. Rendon appear in the preface. The combined readings offer a composite picture of the contemporary Chicano, from his ancestral roots through the last 125 years. The "tomorrow" section analyzes the Movimiento which has stimulated interest in cultural nationalism and raises questions about its viability as a social movement relevant to all Mexican Americans.

CA-6 Forbes, Jack D. AZTECAS DEL NORTE: THE CHICANOS OF AZTLAN. Greenwich, Conn.: Fawcett Publications, 1973. 336 p. Maps. Notes. Pap.

In an introductory essay the author gives recognition to the heritage of Mexico and points out how it is also "... a living part of the past, the present, and the future of the United States." The remainder of the work consists of brief, explanatory notes by the author on excerpts from previously published materials dealing with history, education, acculturation, discrimination, politics, self-identity, and the Chicano's movement toward self-realization. The reader is offered an overview of the Chicano from Indo-hispanic times to the present.

CA-7 Gomez, Rudolph, ed. THE CHANGING MEXICAN AMERICAN: A READER. El Paso: University of Texas at El Paso, 1972. vi, 312 p. Biblio. Tables. Pap.

With the objective of creating more awareness for the presence of the Chicano, the editor has arranged Chicano and Anglo selections from previously printed materials authored by subject specialists and writers under six broad topics. Each part is preceeded by the editor's own introduction. The parts are historical perspective, problems confronted by Chicanos in education, housing, and employment, changes in employment patterns, housing, family, attitudes and political activism, La Raza and political activity, literature, and leaders such as Chavez, Tijerina, and Rodolfo Gonzales. In general the different parts contain adequate selections; however, the one on literature could be strengthened.

CA-8 Grebler, Leo, et al. THE MEXICAN AMERICAN PEOPLE: THE NATION'S SECOND LARGEST MINORITY. New York: Free Press, 1970. 777 p. Apps. Biblio. Index. Graphs. Maps. Tables.

An encyclopedic work based on monographs produced by specialists assisted by graduate students over a four-year period, 1964-68. The focus is on the socioeconomic and political situation of Chicanos in urban areas of the five southwestern states. The headings of the seven parts into which the work is divided give an indication of the coverage: (1) setting, (2) historical perspective, (3) socioeconomic conditions, (4) the individual in the social system, (5) the role of churches, (6) political interaction, and (7) summary and conclusions. The eleven appendices include such supplementary data as that derived on Mexican Americans from the U.S. Census, information on the Los Angeles school study, and the Roman Catholic Church. The sixty-six-page unannotated bibliography lists books, pamphlets, government publications, journal articles, unpublished dissertations, and other unpublished materials. Though already dated in some respects, this work is still one of the most useful reference tools for locating information pertinent to Chicanos.

CA-9 Haddox, John. LOS CHICANOS: AN AWAKENING PEOPLE. Southwestern Studies Monograph, no. 28. Illustrated by Jose Cisneros. University of Texas at El Paso, Texas Western Press, 1970. 44 p. Biblio. B & w draws. Pap.

This concise, authoritative, and well-documented monograph attempts to promote understanding of and appreciation for the values and heritage of the Chicano.

CA-10 McWilliams, Carey. NORTH FROM MEXICO. THE SPANISH-SPEAKING PEOPLE OF THE UNITED STATES. Philadelphia: J.B. Lippincott Co., 1949. 324 p. Biblio. Index. Map.

Considered a classic because until the appearance of this documented work much of what had been written about Mexican Americans by Anglo writers was oftentimes disparaging and less than the truth. Provides an objective historical account beginning with Fray Marcos de Niza, Coronado, Kino, and de Anza, and through the movement northward by the peoples of Mexico who eventually settled mainly in the Southwest. McWilliams traces the origins of discrimination and attempts to analyze racial tensions during the late forties, including the zoot-suit riots. Concludes with a bibliographic essay and chapter notes.

CA-11 Romano-V., Octavio Ignacio, ed. VOICES: READINGS FROM EL GRITO: A JOURNAL OF CONTEMPORARY MEXICAN AMERICAN THOUGHT, 1967 - 1971. Berkeley, Calif.: Quinto Sol Publications, 1971. 211 p. Graphs. Tables. Pap.

The tone of the work is established in the preface by Herminio Rios C.: "We are in the belly of the shark, and the question of whether or not to gut the shark is academic. It is clearly a question of method." The content is arranged in four parts: (1) Stereotypes and the Distortion of History, (2) The Chicano Struggle, (3) Education, and (4) Chicanos in the Modern State. As a unit the book represents one of the best samplings of Chicano thought.

CA-12 Rosaldo, Renato, et al., eds. CHICANO: THE EVOLUTION OF A PEOPLE. Minneapolis: Winston Press, 1973. 461 p. B & w draws. Pap.

Another reader of reprinted material organized into six sections: (1) Beginnings of a People, (2) Acquiescence and Adjustment, (3) Trying to Crack the System, (4) The Beginnings of Bronze Power, (5) The Urban Experience, and (6) Conclusion. Since there are few original writings about Chicanos by Chicanos, the same familiar names reappear. The selections are not restricted to those of Mexican American writers. Hence, the work opens with a chapter from the old standby, Carey McWilliams' NORTH FROM MEXICO (see item CA-10). Recommended for the college and university student as an introduction to more in-depth reading.

CA-13 Sanchez, George I. FORGOTTEN PEOPLE: A STUDY OF NEW MEXICANS. Albuquerque: University of New Mexico Press, 1940. viii, 98 p. B & w photos. Tables.

The first of its kind to be written by a Mexican American, this narrative dramatizes the socioeconomic plight of the people of New Mexico. As an educator, Sanchez combines factual information with insights gained over the many years he worked and lived among the

"forgotten people" whom he loved and wished to help.
With slight variation, the author's findings of thirty-four
years ago still hold true today.

CA-14 Simmen, Edward, ed., PAIN AND PROMISE: THE CHICANO TODAY.
Introduction by editor. New York: New American Library, Mentor
Book, 1972. 362 p. Biblio. Essay.

A number of previously published essays, together with
several speeches and reports, have been organized to
respond to these questions about Chicanos: (1) Who are
these "discontented" Americans? (2) Why the discon-
tentment? (3) What have they done to attract the attention of the Anglo majority? (4) How will Chicanos
correct the situation in our society? Not all the writings are of equal literary importance, but they fulfill
the editor's objective of presenting different views and
approaches by both Anglos and Chicanos. The work is
supplemented with a bibliographic essay.

CA-15 Steiner, Stan. LA RAZA: THE MEXICAN AMERICANS. New York:
Harper & Row Publishers, 1969. xii, 418 p. Biblio. sources p. 393.
B & w photos. Index.

Panoramic view of the Mexican Americans as revealed
through interviews with numerous personalities such as
Tijerina, Chavez, Luis Valdez, and "Corky" Gonzales.
The sensitivity of the author in capturing the essence of
Mexican American life in the United States today makes
this an important "read first" book on Chicanos.

CA-16 Stoddard, Ellwyn R. MEXICAN AMERICANS. Ethnic Groups in Comparative Perspective. Foreword by Peter I. Rose. New York: Random House,
1973. 269 p. Biblio. Index. Pap.

Unlike some previous authors who have produced works
of this type, this Anglo American scholar has made a
genuine attempt to present an accurate, synthesized
study of the cultural heritage and experience of the
Chicano. In addition to providing historical background,
he also deals with the problems of identity, differences
in cultural values, education, economics, and the efforts
which nurtured the Movimiento and gave rise to Chicanismo.

CA-17 U.S. Inter-Agency Committee on Mexican American Affairs. THE MEXI-
CAN AMERICAN: A NEW FOCUS ON OPPORTUNITY. TESTIMONY
PRESENTED AT THE CABINET COMMITTEE HEARINGS ON MEXICAN
AMERICAN AFFAIRS. EL PASO, TEXAS. OCTOBER 26-28, 1967.
Washington, D.C.: Government Printing Office, 1968. 267 p. Graphs.
Tables. Pap.

Included are the fifty-one statements that were presented
by Chicano men and women from different walks of life.
The papers are grouped under the following categories:
agriculture, labor, health, education and welfare, housing
and urban development, war on poverty, and economic
and social development. These statements are of particular importance not only because of their unique presentation before high government officials, but also because
they represent the thoughts voiced at a time when the
Mexican American population had reached a peak of
frustration. The problems and inner feelings long suppressed were disclosed, together with what Chicanos
expected the government to do in order to improve the
socioeconomic and political situation of Mexican Americans.

Education

Bibliography

CB-1 Altus, David M., comp. MEXICAN AMERICAN EDUCATION, A SE-
LECTED BIBLIOGRAPHY. SUPPLEMENT, no. 1. Las Cruces, N. Mex.:
Educational Resources Information Center (ERIC). Clearinghouse on Rural Education and Small Schools (CRESS). New Mexico State University,
1971. 206 p.

A supplement to MEXICAN AMERICAN EDUCATION, A
SELECTED BIBLIOGRAPHY (see CB-5). Cites speeches,
conference papers, reports, pamphlets, theses, etc., concerning the education of Mexican American children and
adults. Bilingual education and English as a second
language are among the subjects stressed. The work is
divided into two parts. The first contains more than
150 citations and abstracts which have appeared in RE-
SEARCH IN EDUCATION (RIE) from June 1969 through
December 1970. Part two includes twenty-three citations which have appeared in CURRENT INDEX TO
JOURNALS IN EDUCATION (CIJE) from January 1969
through June 1970. Includes ordering information and
RIE and CIJE subject indexes.

CB-2 Charles, Edgar B., ed. MEXICAN AMERICAN EDUCATION: A BIB-
LIOGRAPHY. Las Cruces, N. Mex.: Educational Resources Information
Center (ERIC). Clearinghouse on Rural Education and Small Schools
(CRESS). New Mexico State University, 1968. iv, 22 p. Pap.

Prepared for the 1968 National Conference on Educational
Opportunities for Mexican Americans held in Austin,
Texas, this subject bibliography is especially useful as
it is annotated and includes ninety select items made up

of books, monographs, journal articles, and a few unpublished materials. The materials listed are subdivided
among six subject headings: pre-school education,
elementary, secondary, higher, adult, and migrant education. Ordering information is provided for items
available through ERIC.

CB-3 Colorado. Adams State College. Alamosa. Center for Cultural Studies.
KNOWING AND EDUCATING THE DISADVANTAGED: AN ANNOTA-
TED BIBLIOGRAPHY. Alamosa, Colo.: 1965. 460 p.

The disadvantaged referred to in the title are the agricultural migratory workers among whom are many Chicanos. The bibliography is divided into three parts:
a topic index with main entries alphabetized by title
under classified headings; main entries including general, periodical, and audiovisual materials; and a publishers' directory, resource and service sources, together
with an A-V materials producers index. Not an especially easy tool to use, but since it does include some
materials relevant to Mexican Americans, researchers
may find it worthwhile to examine its bibliographic
content. Citations include references to topics such
as acculturation and bilingualism.

CB-4 El Paso, Texas. El Paso Public Schools. BILINGUAL MATERIALS: A
LISTING FOR LIBRARY RESOURCE CENTERS. El Paso: 1974. 79 p.
Apps. Pap.

Teachers and school librarians working primarily with
Chicanitos will no longer be able to say that they lack
information on available materials to support bilingual
and intercultural programs, for this annotated listing--
intended for school librarians in the El Paso Public
School System--uncovers a wealth of possibilities.
The items are identified by type of medium (filmstrips,
recordings, kits, slides, transparencies, games, models,
and books), and by such information as title, producer,
date of publication, contents, price, source, suggested
Dewey classification, grade level, and recommendation.
The appendixes list sources and evaluators, several of
whom are of Spanish surname.

CB-5 Heathman, James E., and Martinez, Cecilia, comps. MEXICAN AMERI-
CAN EDUCATION, A SELECTED BIBLIOGRAPHY. Las Cruces, N. Mex.:
Educational Resources Information Center (ERIC). Clearinghouse on Rural Education and Small Schools (CRESS). New Mexico State University, 1969. 59 p. Index. Pap. Sold by Government Printing Office.

Contains citations which have appeared in RESEARCH IN
EDUCATION (RIE) through June 1969. Not all are concerned with Chicanos, as the title suggests. Several deal

with native Americans and Blacks. Citations are followed by descriptive terms to describe content of publication. Some are much too broad to be of any use.
Frequently-used descriptors are language instruction,
Spanish culture, bilingualism, inter-group relations,
behavior problems, migrant children, and English (second language). Prices provided for microfiche and
hard-copy reproductions. The subject index is arranged
alphabetically by the descriptive terms.

CB-6 Link, Albert D., comp. MEXICAN AMERICAN EDUCATION, A SE-
LECTED BIBLIOGRAPHY (WITH ERIC ABSTRACTS). ERIC/CRESS SUPPLE-
MENT, no. 2. Las Cruces, N. Mex.: Educational Resources Informa-
tion Center (ERIC). Clearinghouse on Rural Education and Small Schools
(CRESS). New Mexico State University, 1972. 345 p.

Supplement no. 2 is basically the same as Supplement
no. 1 (see CB-1). The difference is in coverage.
Part I includes citations and abstracts which appeared
in RIE from January 1971 through March 1972. Part
II contains citations which appeared in CIJE from June
1970 through March 1972. Separate RIE and CIJE subject indexes are included as Part III.

CB-7 MIGRANT EDUCATION, A SELECTED BIBLIOGRAPHY (WITH ERIC AB-
STRACTS). ERIC/CRESS SUPPLEMENT, no. 3. Las Cruces, N. Mex.:
Educational Resources Information Center (ERIC), Clearinghouse on Rural
Education and Small Schools (CRESS). New Mexico State University,
1973. vii, 159 p. Sold by Government Printing Office.

A three-part work. The first includes citations and abstracts which have appeared in RESEARCH IN EDUCA-
TION (RIE) from April 1971 through September 1972.
Part two contains citations in CURRENT INDEX TO
JOURNALS IN EDUCATION (CIJE) from December
1970 through September 1972. Part three consists of
the RIE and CIJE subject index. The material cited
includes books, periodical articles, reports, booklets,
and any other publication which contains information
on migrants, particularly those dealing with their education. While only a limited number of citations are
directly concerned with Chicanos, they do include many
references to subjects pertinent to their education, e.g.,
bilingualism, child care, cultural differences, English
as a second language, preschool education, and early
childhood education.

Only the most recent supplement was selected for inclusion. The reader may wish to know that three previous
ERIC/CRESS publications have been issued. The basic
work, MIGRANT EDUCATION, A SELECTED BIBLIO-
GRAPHY (Ed 028 011), was published in 1961; Supple-

ment no. 1 (ED 040 002), 1970; and Supplement no. 2 (ED 055 706), 1971.

CB-8   Navarro, Eliseo G. THE CHICANO COMMUNITY: A SELECTED BIB-
LIOGRAPHY FOR USE IN SOCIAL WORK EDUCATION. New York:
Council on Social Work Education, 1971. 57 p.

Designed to provide resource material for social work
students and faculty. This critically annotated listing
covers topics such as historical background, acculturation, education, health and welfare, religion, politics,
economics, and literature. Each entry is preceded by
code letter indicating subject matter of material. (An
expansion of Navarro's 1969 bibliography [see CA-1].)

CB-9   Sanchez, George I., and Putnam, Howard. MATERIALS RELATING TO
THE EDUCATION OF SPANISH-SPEAKING PEOPLE IN THE UNITED
STATES: AN ANNOTATED BIBLIOGRAPHY. Austin: University of Tex-
as, 1959. 76 p. Index. Pap.

Contains 882 numbered references to books, articles,
monographs, bulletins, courses of study, bibliographies,
unpublished theses, and dissertations, arranged alphabetically by author with brief annotations. Subject index
has cross references.

CB-10 U.S. Department of Health, Education and Welfare. Office of Education. ERIC CATALOG OF SELECTED DOCUMENTS ON THE DISAD-
VANTAGED. Number and Author Index. Washington, D.C.: Government Printing Office, 1966. 130 p.

Lists 1,740 documents available in microfiche through
the Educational Resources Information Center (ERIC).
Entries consist of bibliographical citations, abstracts,
and a list of descriptive index terms. Divided into
two sections: (1) by document number, and (2) alphabetically by author. Companion volume is a word list
of index names.

CB-11 Weinberg, Meyer. THE EDUCATION OF THE MINORITY CHILD: A
COMPREHENSIVE BIBLIOGRAPHY OF 10,000 SELECTED ENTRIES. Chicago: Integrated Education Associates, 1970. 530 p.

Essentially concerned with Blacks, but includes references to Mexican Americans in California, New Mexico,
and Texas. Books, articles, and theses arranged by
author. Reflects the literature of the past seventy years.
ERIC (Educational Resources Information Center) numbers
and prices given. Brief annotations and author index.

Directories

CB-12 U.S. Cabinet Committee on Opportunity for the Spanish Speaking. SPAN-ISH SURNAMED AMERICAN COLLEGE GRADUATES, 1971-72. 2 parts. Washington, D.C.: Government Printing Office, 1971. Pap.

Intended as a recruiting directory for employers; more than 800 colleges and universities are listed alphabetically by state. Within this listing the work provides names of graduates, their respective disciplines and date of graduation. Separate tables furnish the total number of students graduating in the various disciplines as well as the total number of graduates. Part II includes data received after the deadline for part I, and also information relative to graduates from Miami-Dade Junior College of Florida.

Education

CB-13 Brussell, Charles B. DISADVANTAGED MEXICAN AMERICAN CHILD-REN AND EARLY EDUCATION EXPERIENCE. Austin, Tex.: Southwest Educational Development Corporation, 1968. vi, 105 p. Biblio. Pap.

Described as a synthesis of the literature and also as a bibliography. However, the more appropriate term is the first one, since it is not a bibliography in the traditional sense of the word. The emphasis is on early educational experience as presented in the literature written since 1950. The material is arranged into six parts; the last one constitutes a summary. Others deal with history and demography, social characteristics, psychological characteristics, education of young children, and the ongoing and anticipated educational projects concerned with early childhood. A bibliography divided into five parts corresponds to the respective sections of the monograph.

CB-14 Cabrera, Ysidro Arturo. A STUDY OF AMERICAN AND MEXICAN-AMERICAN CULTURE VALUES AND THEIR SIGNIFICANCE IN EDUCA-TION. Thesis, University of Colorado, 1963. Reprint. San Francisco: R and E Research Associates, 1972. v, 203 p. Biblio.

Information on cultural values of middle-class Anglos and Mexican Americans has been synthesized with the idea that if teachers are aware of the compatibility and incompatibility of the two-culture system they will be better able to plan suitable curricula and develop programs of education to fulfill the needs of Spanish-speaking children. The work is complemented by a study of European and Mexican immigrations which provides understanding of the acculturation processes of the groups

involved. The findings show that typical problems of
immigrant adjustment were culture conflict, prejudices
and discrimination, and parent-children conflicts. The
data for this study is derived from both published and
nonpublished materials.

CB-15 Carter, Thomas P. MEXICAN AMERICANS IN SCHOOL: A HISTORY
OF EDUCATIONAL NEGLECT. New York: College Entrance Examina-
tion Board, 1970. 235 p. Biblio. Tables.

A thorough analysis of the role of education in the
lives of Chicanos. The author begins with the history
of problems and influences inherent in the school system
and progresses through the dismal failure of the schools
to assess the needs of the Mexican American student.
Mexican American reactions to school and community,
as well as special school programs for children such as
English as a second language and bilingual curricula
are explored.

CB-16 Castaneda, Alfredo, et al., eds. MEXICAN AMERICANS AND EDUCA-
TIONAL CHANGE. New York: Arno Press, 1974. 424 p.

Includes seventeen papers presented at the symposium on
"Mexican Americans and Educational Change" held at
the University of California at Riverside, May 21-22,
1971. The thrust of the writings is to explore solutions
to those problems which have over the years retarded
the education of Chicanos, particularly in early childhood. The schools are indicted by the late George I.
Sanchez, the renowned New Mexican educator, and
other educators point out where the schools have failed
and why change must take place. Subsequent papers
are concerned with the challenge to biculturalism and
bilingual education. Some contributors are Armando
Rodriguez, Carlos E. Cortez, Mark Hanson, Armando
Navarro, Henry M. Ramirez, Thomas P. Carter, Atilano A. Valencia, Horacio Ulibarri, and Albar A. Pena.
Of special interest to educators working with Chicanos
and other culturally different groups.

CB-17 Davidson, Walter Craig. THE MEXICAN AMERICAN HIGH SCHOOL
GRADUATE OF LAREDO. Laredo, Tex.: Federal Projects, Laredo Independent School District, 1971. 203 p. Apps. Maps. Available
from ERIC, Counseling and Personnel Services Information Center, 611
Church Street, Ann Arbor, Michigan 48104.

By eliciting information from the 1965 and 1969 graduates
of a barrio high school, the author ascertains what in
the opinion of the students needs to be done to make
sensible changes in the public school setting to increase

the rate and degree of success for future graduates.
Based on the outcome of this study, several recommendations worth considering are made. Heading the list is
the establishment of a guidance and counseling department "to insure better institutional support for each
student." Extensive appendices include among other
items the responses of forty-nine principals and teachers
to the question, "What in your opinion is the single
most important barrier to success for the typical Mexican American of Laredo?"

CB-18 De Hoyos, Arturo. OCCUPATIONAL AND EDUCATIONAL LEVELS OF
ASPIRATION OF MEXICAN-AMERICAN YOUTH. Thesis, Michigan State
University, 1961. Reprint. San Francisco: R and E Research Associates,
1971. 146 p. Apps. Pap.

Is there an association between the Chicano's aspirations
and levels of occupation and education? Is there a relationship between socioeconomic factors and acculturation? To answer these and related questions the author
prepared and administered a special questionnaire which
was completed by students in two public junior high
schools and two parochial schools in Lansing, Michigan.
The data revealed a high level of occupational and educational aspirations among Chicanos in this area. Also,
their socioeconomic status is higher than was the case
when they lived in the Southwest or when they worked
as migrants. The author believes that in general Chicanos in the northern part of the United States are becoming acculturated at a faster pace than they are in
the Southwest.

CB-19 Edington, Everett D. RECRUITMENT OF SPANISH-SPEAKING STUDENTS
INTO HIGHER EDUCATION. Long Beach: California State College,
1969. 20 p. Pap.

How to get more Mexican Americans into colleges and
universities is the principal concern of the author. He
outlines the problem and suggests solutions.

CB-20 Escobedo, Arturo E. CHICANO COUNSELOR. CONSEJERO AT THE
CROSSROADS. Illus. by Hector F. De Leon. Lubbock, Tex.: Truchas
Publications, 1974. viii, 211 p. B & w photos. Pap.

The Colorado-born Chicano consejero enthusiastically
tells about his experiences that began ten years ago in
a junior high school. Presently he is counselor in the
Denver Public Schools. The message is that there is a
definite need for Chicano counselors, but these professionals must identify and genuinely relate to students.
They must be willing to put aside their paperwork and

allow time to listen to what students have to say. By describing specific cases and activities, the author shows that students can be motivated in different manners by getting them involved in writing poetry, skits, or by making use of the guitar. His success stems from treating students as individuals, being cognizant of their needs, and knowing how to instill confidence and pride in their persons. This is not a scholarly work, but Chicanos and non-Chicanos could profit from Escobedo's experiences.

CB-21 Farmer, George L. EDUCATION: THE DILEMMA OF THE SPANISH-SURNAME AMERICAN. Los Angeles: School of Education, University of Southern California, 1968. ii, 55 p. Biblio. Tables.

Although not an in-depth study, it does furnish data on various areas of social conflict which have an impact on the educational achievement level of Mexican Americans, i.e., history, differences in values, religion, language, housing, employement, and education. This work is specifically concerned with attitudes and practices in the Los Angeles area, but much of the information provided is also applicable to Chicanos in other parts of the country. Includes recommendations to teachers.

CB-22 Forbes, Jack D. MEXICAN-AMERICANS: A HANDBOOK FOR EDUCATORS. Berkeley, Calif.: Far West Laboratory for Educational Research and Development, 1970. 34 p. Biblio. Pap. Sold by Government Printing Office.

A sketch of who are the Mexican Americans--past and present--as well as suggestions for teachers and administrators on supplementary materials for classroom use. While this publication is useful as an informational-type pamphlet for the novice, is inadequate as a handbook for educators.

CB-23 Grebler, Leo. THE SCHOOLING GAP: SIGNS OF PROGRESS. Mexican American Study Project. Advance Report, no. 7. Los Angeles: Division of Research, Graduate School of Business Administration, University of California, 1967. vii, 48 p. Apps. Graphs. Tables. Pap.

This report statistically details the glaring, known gap in formal schooling which exists between Chicanos and Anglos as well as "nonwhites." Findings indicate that in 1960 southwestern adult Chicanos averaged 7.1 years of schooling whereas adult Anglos averaged 12.1 and "nonwhites" 9.0. The distressing part is that there is evidence of only moderate progress. This moderate progress had an encouraging aspect, however, in that the educational standing of Chicanos improved, though slowly, at a time when federal aid and anti-poverty programs were not available.

CB-24 Guerra, Manuel H. THE RETENTION OF MEXICAN AMERICAN STU-
DENTS IN HIGHER EDUCATION WITH SPECIAL REFERENCE TO BICUL-
TURAL AND BILINGUAL PROBLEMS. Published for the National Training Program for Teachers, Counselors, and Administrators Involved in the
Recruitment, Retention, and Financial Assistance of Mexican Americans
in Higher Education. Long Beach: California State College, 1969. 27
p. Biblio. Pap.

> The bilingual and bicultural problems which have handi-
> capped Chicanos from the barrios in their earlier school
> years are identified as the most difficult obstacles to
> higher education. Being bilingual and bicultural does
> have advantages, but the assets of these students have
> passed unperceived and unappreciated by tradition-minded
> educators. The answer to retention and motivation of
> the Chicano college student lies in giving recognition
> to his bilingual and bicultural background and by pro-
> viding financial aid.

CB-25 Hernandez, Deluvina. MEXICAN AMERICAN CHALLENGE TO A SACRED
COW. Chicano Studies Center Monograph, no. 1. Los Angeles: Azt-
lan Publications, University of California, 1970. viii, 60 p. Biblio.
Pap.

> Through a systematic critique, the author challenges two
> reports prepared by the University of California Graduate
> School of Education which deal with the educational
> achievements and aspirations of urban Mexican American
> youth and their values and achievements as compared
> with Anglos. The critique attempts to show how social
> scientists have been guilty of perpetuating the very ste-
> reotypic concepts which research is supposed to expose.

CB-26 THE INVISIBLE MINORITY. REPORT OF THE NEA-TUCSON SURVEY
ON THE TEACHING OF SPANISH TO THE SPANISH-SPEAKING. Washington, D.C.: Department of Rural Education, National Education Association, 1966. vii, 39 p. Apps. Pap.

> As is pointed out in the report, this is not a research
> study in the formal sense. Instead it reflects the obser-
> vations of a group of Spanish-speaking educators who
> visited elementary and secondary public schools in the
> Southwest which had innovative programs designed to
> meet the needs of Mexican American students. The em-
> phasis is clearly on the importance of bilingualism. A
> succinct picture of the Chicano child makes up the first
> portion of the report. The appendix lists the individual
> schools and school systems visited.

CB-27 Johnson, Henry Sioux, and Hernandez-M., William J. EDUCATING
THE MEXICAN AMERICAN. Valley Forge, Pa.: Judson Press, 1970.
384 p. Biblio. Index. Notes. Tables. Pap.

> Made up primarily of reprinted selections authored by
> both Anglo and Mexican American writers. Views are
> expressed on a broad range of topics pertaining to the
> education of Mexican Americans in the Southwest, such
> as acculturation, nonverbal tests of intelligence, reten-
> tion of students, educational needs of migrant children,
> teacher training, and bicultural and bilingual instruction.
> The stress is on the latter aspects of education.

CB-28 Linn, George Byron. A STUDY OF SEVERAL LINGUISTIC FUNCTIONS
OF MEXICAN-AMERICAN CHILDREN IN A TWO-LANGUAGE ENVIR-
ONMENT. Thesis, University of Southern California, 1965. Reprint.
San Francisco: R and E Research Associates, 1971. viii, 120 p. Bib-
lio. Tables. Pap.

> To study the language development of children (seventh
> and eighth graders) in a bilingual-bicultural environment,
> the author studied three groups of children in southern
> California: (1) Chicanos who had spoken both English
> and Spanish when they entered kindergarten, (2) mono-
> lingual Anglos, and (3) Chicanos who had spoken only
> English, but whose parents communicated in English and
> Spanish. The findings indicated that the monolingual
> child generally made a better showing in linguistic func-
> tioning than the bilingual child.

CB-29 Litsinger, Dolores Escobar. THE CHALLENGE OF TEACHING MEXICAN-
AMERICAN STUDENTS. New York: American Book Co., 1973. 222
p. Apps. Index. Graphs. Tables. Pap.

> A timely book for educators who are still exploring ways
> and means to improve the education of Chicanos. Theo-
> ries are dealt with to a minimum degree. The author,
> a professor of education, concentrates on the practical
> aspects of teaching. She suggests strategies which make
> use of the student's language and his bicultural back-
> ground. A plea is made for relevant curriculum which
> will focus on the needs of Mexican American students
> as well as improved instruments and techniques to assess
> the student's potential. Stress is also placed on reforms
> concerned with teacher training. Sample lesson plans
> in English and Spanish are included. The appendices
> provide information on programs for migratory children,
> bilingual/bicultural education programs already in opera-
> tion in several states, and teaching techniques during
> the aural-oral phase.

CB-30 Lopez, Richard Emilio. ANXIETY, ACCULTURATION AND THE URBAN

CHICANO: THE RELATIONSHIP BETWEEN STAGES OF ACCULTURA-TION AND ANXIETY LEVEL OF EOP STUDENTS. Berkeley, Calif.: California Book Co., 1970. 41 p. Apps. Refs. Pap.

> Suggests that Chicano EOP (Economic Opportunity Pro-gram) freshmen at San Jose State College are at many stages of acculturation and that anxiety levels seem to be highest among those Chicanos unwilling to attempt cultural transfer.

CB-31 Manuel, Herschel T. THE EDUCATION OF MEXICAN AND SPANISH-SPEAKING CHILDREN IN TEXAS. Austin: Fund for Research in the Social Sciences, University of Texas, 1930. ix, 173 p. App. Biblio. B & w photos. Graphs. Tables.

> This study can best serve as a historical reference to the time of segregated schools when instruction was conduct-ed by an all-English method and tests of intelligence and school achievement made no provisions for the stu-dent's mother tongue or cultural background. Several of the problems cited, such as enrollment and attend-ance, still persist. Therefore, those seriously interested in the education of Mexican Americans are encouraged to seek sources with updated information.

CB-32 Montez, Philip. MEXICANISMO VS. RETENTION. IMPLICATIONS OF RETAINING MEXICAN AMERICAN STUDENTS IN HIGHER EDUCATION. Long Beach: California State College, 1969. 18 p. Biblio. Pap.

> The author reviews some past and present efforts to re-tain Mexican Americans in higher education and makes recommendations for future planning and programming from the point of view of an educational psychologist.

CB-33 National Conference on Educational Opportunities for Mexican Americans, Austin, Texas, 1968. PROCEEDINGS. Austin: Southwest Educational Development Laboratory, [1969?]. 130 p. B & w photos. Pap.

> The addresses (or their abstracts) delivered by Harold Howe II, Armando Rodriguez, John Hughes, James A. Turman, Nolan Estes, and Ralph Yarborough make up the major portion of this work. The focus is on the way schools and some organizations are resolving prob-lems concerned with the education of Chicanos. Bilin-ual education and the schooling of migrant children are emphasized. Summaries of the discussion groups and of various bilingual programs which are operating in dif-ferent parts of the country are included.

CB-34 Parr, Eunice Elvira. A COMPARATIVE STUDY OF MEXICAN AND AMERICAN CHILDREN IN THE SCHOOLS OF SAN ANTONIO, TEXAS.

Dissertation, University of Chicago, 1926. Reprint. San Francisco: R and E Research Associates, 1971. ix, 52 p. App. Graphs. Tables. Pap.

Should "Mexican" children be segregated into separate schools, taught in the same way as Anglo children, or can a child profit by studying in a mixed school which allows association with English-speaking children? In seeking an answer the author selected three elementary schools in San Antonio because of "its proximity to Mexico": one "purely Mexican," one "purely American," and one of mixed enrollment. Better scholastic achievement appeared in the "Mexican" school leading the author to conclude "...that for the good of Mexican children they should be separated from the American children in the schools."

CB-35 EL PLAN DE SANTA BARBARA: A CHICANO PLAN FOR HIGHER EDUCATION. Analyses and Positions by the Chicano Coordinating Council on Higher Education. Santa Barbara, Calif.: La Causa Publications, 1970. 154 p. Biblio. B & w draws. and photos.

These guidelines are designed to give other Chicanos information on such matters as Chicano studies programs, recruitments, admissions, curriculum, and political action on the decision-making processes of universities, community organizations, and noncommunity institutions which affect Mexican Americans.

CB-36 Pollack, Erwin W., and Menacker, Julius. SPANISH-SPEAKING STUDENTS AND GUIDANCE. Guidance Monograph Series. Boston: Houghton Mifflin Co., 1971. xi, 86 p. Biblio. Index. Pap.

Chicanos and Puerto Ricans are the Spanish-speaking students under consideration. While similarities and differences are discussed, each group is treated separately. Aware that the traditional school practices and techniques of guidance offered to students who are culturally different have met with little or no success, the authors advocate that the cultural strengths which these students bring to school be accentuated to meet their educational needs. Bilingualism and bicultural experiences should be considered positive attributes which can enrich their education in school and beyond. The book is designed for educators and, in particular, for counselors who work with students from these ethnic groups.

CB-37 Reynolds, Annie. THE EDUCATION OF SPANISH-SPEAKING CHILDREN IN FIVE SOUTHWESTERN STATES. Bulletin 1933, no. 11. United States Department of the Interior, Office of Education. Washington, D.C.: Superintendent of Documents, 1933. 64 p. Biblio. Tables. Pap.

The report is dated, but it may help explain why adult
Chicanos today average eight years of schooling in comparison to the twelve years averaged by adult Anglos.
The matter of intelligence, educational achievement,
and school progress of Chicanos forms a significant part
of this work. Of special interest are the advanced
ideas of the New Mexican educator, George I. Sanchez,
that came into fruition in later years; namely, that
language and environment are important factors to be
considered in the I.Q. of Spanish-speaking pupils.
Statistical information is drawn from the reports issued
by the U.S. Bureau of the Census, 1890-1930.

CB-38 Sanchez, George I. CONCERNING SEGREGATION OF SPANISH-
SPEAKING CHILDREN IN THE PUBLIC SCHOOLS. Inter-American Education Occasional Papers, no. IX. Austin: University of Texas, 1951.
75 p. App. Pap.

The author summarizes his condemnation of the segregation of Spanish-speaking children in the public schools.
He shows that no justification for it could be found
among competent educational authorities. Details about
the two cases which played an important part in the
conclusive legal decisions on the subject, the Mendez
case in California, and the Delgado case in Texas, are
included. The courts decided that to segregate Spanish-
speaking children in the public schools was a violation
of their rights guaranteed by the U.S. Constitution.
The appendix contains abstracts of the principal features
of these two cases.

CB-39 Stevens, Larry. MEXICAN AMERICANS IN CALIFORNIA. 2nd. rev.
ed. Stockton, Calif.: Hammer Press, Relevant Instructional Materials,
1970. 40 p. Pap.

A pamphlet prepared for the purpose of providing the
classroom teacher and students with information about
the contributions of Mexican Americans to the development of California. Also available in Spanish. Among
the topics included are early landholdings, the discovery
of gold, agriculture, the building of railroads, and labor strikes.

CB-40 Takesian, Sarkis Armen. A COMPARATIVE STUDY OF THE MEXICAN-
AMERICAN GRADUATE AND DROPOUT. Dissertation, School of Education, University of Southern California, 1967. Reprint. San Francisco:
R and E Research Associates, 1971. vii, 131 p. Apps. Biblio. Tables. Pap.

One hundred and two young Chicano students from the
same high school district in Southern California were
studied to determine why some of them dropped out of

64

school while others graduated. The most common reason
given for quitting school was to go to work. A large
number also dropped out after reaching legal age. Fe-
males showed a higher dropout rate than males. Graduates liked school and felt they were liked by their
teachers. By contrast, dropouts did not participate in
class discussion due to lack of self-confidence and inadequate communication skills, and they generally felt
their school experience was not pleasant. Graduates,
in turn, were readers and enjoyed superior speaking
abilities. The author concludes with a number of recommendations.

CB-41 Tireman, Loyd Spencer. TEACHING SPANISH SPEAKING CHILDREN.
Rev. ed. Albuquerque: University of New Mexico Press, 1951. 252
p. Index.

Although outdated in some respects, this comprehensive
study on bilingualism contains useful information for
those working with native Spanish-speaking children.
One chapter is devoted to the concept of a community
school as a means of attracting and keeping the Spanish-
speaking child in school.

CB-42 U.S. Commission on Civil Rights. ETHNIC ISOLATION OF MEXICAN
AMERICANS IN THE PUBLIC SCHOOLS OF THE SOUTHWEST. Mexican
American Education Study Report, no. 1. April, 1971. Washington,
D.C.: 1971. 102 p. Apps. Graphs. B & w photos. Maps. Tables.
Pap. Sold by Government Printing Office.

Findings show that Chicano students in the Southwest
are isolated in predominantly Mexican American districts.
The problem is especially severe in Texas and New
Mexico with California having the least imbalanced
schools. Findings also document the gross underrepresentation of Chicanos in the schools' professional staffs.
Chicano principals, vice-principals, and librarians are
represented in even smaller numbers than teachers. Representation of Mexican Americans on boards of education is also lacking. In effect, with the exception of
custodians and teachers' aides, Chicano professionals
form a very small part of the public schools' staffs
throughout the Southwest and are limited in particular
to schools with enrollments of eighty percent or more
Mexican Americans.

CB-43 _____. THE EXCLUDED STUDENT. EDUCATIONAL PRACTICES AF-
FECTING MEXICAN AMERICANS IN THE SOUTHWEST. Mexican American Education Study Report, no. 3. May 1972. Washington, D.C.:
1972. 86 p. Apps. B & w photos. Graphs. Tables. Pap. Sold by
Government Printing Office.

This report documents that the practice of cultural exclusion in Southwest schools is responsible for failure of Chicano students to develop as full participants in the American life. Findings disclose that there is suppression of the Spanish language, exclusion of the Mexican heritage, and little or no involvement of parents and the Mexican American community. Of the three deterrents cited, the suppression of Spanish appears to be the most serious since this is the mother tongue for nearly fifty percent of the Mexican American first graders. The report mentions that until practices and policies are instituted to correct the prevailing situation, equal opportunity in education for Raza people will continue to remain a myth rather than a reality.

CB-44 _____ . METHODOLOGICAL APPENDIX OF RESEARCH METHODS EMPLOYED IN THE MEXICAN AMERICAN EDUCATION STUDY. Washington, D.C.: 1972. v, 156 p. App. Pap. Sold by Government Printing Office.

A study initiated in 1968 by the Commission to determine the status of Mexican American students in a random sampling of school districts in the Southwest. It was conducted in three phases: (1) analysis of HEW data from the fall, 1968, elementary and secondary school survey; (2) analysis of acquired data through a mail survey; and (3) field study. Discloses detailed information on each of these phases.

CB-45 _____ . MEXICAN AMERICAN EDUCATION IN TEXAS: A FUNCTION OF WEALTH. Mexican American Education Study Report, no. 4. August 1972. Washington, D.C.: 1972. 53 p. Apps. Graphs. Tables. Pap. Sold by Government Printing Office.

Examines the revenue sources for educational expenditures in Texas and concludes that Chicanos "are not receiving a financial return commensurate with the drain of their pocketbook." As much as $484 per pupil is spent in districts with a low Chicano density, but as little as $296 per pupil is spent in districts which have a high percentage of Mexican Americans, despite their higher tax rates. The explanation is a system which makes it possible to apportion less monies to educate Chicanitos than Anglo children. A federal court recently declared the system unconstitutional.

CB-46 _____ . TEACHERS AND STUDENTS: DIFFERENCES IN TEACHER INTERACTION WITH MEXICAN AMERICAN AND ANGLO STUDENTS. Mexican American Education Study Report, no. 5. March 1973. Washington, D.C.: 1973. 68 p. Apps. B & w photos. Graphs. Tables. Pap. Sold by Government Printing Office.

Reveals that teachers respond positively to Anglo students to a much greater extent than they do to Chicanos. The latter students also have fewer questions asked of them in the classroom and receive significantly less overall attention from their teachers. This disparity in teacher behavior is pointed out as a factor which has affected the educational opportunities and achievement of Chicano pupils. Language and cultural differences can be offered as an explanation, but not as justification. In the end, then, it is not the children who are failing in the Southwest, but rather the schools and teachers.

CB-47 _____. TOWARD QUALITY EDUCATION FOR MEXICAN AMERICANS. SCHOOL. Mexican American Education Study Report, no. 6. February 1974. Washington, D.C.: 1974. x, 269 p. Apps. Tables. Pap. Sold by Government Printing Office.

Why have schools in the Southwest failed to provide equal educational opportunity to Chicanos? This study examines five specific areas: curriculum, school policies on grade retention, ability grouping, teacher education, and counseling. The findings show conditions and practices to be so inadequate that they are described as "a systematic failure of the educational process, which not only ignores the educational needs of Chicano students but also suppresses their culture and stifles their hopes and ambitions." Specific recommendations are made.

CB-48 _____. THE UNFINISHED EDUCATION: OUTCOMES FOR MINORITIES IN THE FIVE SOUTHWESTERN STATES. Mexican American Educational Series Report, no. 2. October 1971. Washington, D.C.: 1971. 101 p. Apps. B & w photos. Graphs. Tables. Pap. Sold by Government Printing Office.

How successful are schools in the Southwest with regard to the education of their students, and in particular students of ethnic groups? This study evaluates educational achievement in terms of these factors: school holding power, reading skills, grade repetition, overageness, and participation in extracurricular activities. The findings confirm that Blacks, Chicanos, and Indians do not receive the benefits of public education to the same degree as Anglo students. It was found that a large proportion of minority students end up as dropouts. Factors related to their negative school experience are poor reading ability, grade repetition, and overageness. Their participation in extracurricular activities is also much less than is true for their Anglo counterparts.

CB-49 Valencia, Atilano A. BILINGUAL/BICULTURAL EDUCATION: A PER-

SPECTIVE MODEL IN MULTICULTURAL AMERICA. Albuquerque, N. Mex.: Southwestern Cooperative Educational Laboratory, 1969. 21 p. Illus.

>   The author emphasizes that demographic data and a careful examination of the educational needs of the children with Spanish surnames is necessary in ascertaining the desired type of programs for a particular geographical area.

CB-50 _____. IDENTIFICATION AND ASSESSMENT OF ONGOING EDUCATIONAL AND COMMUNITY PROGRAMS FOR SPANISH-SPEAKING PEOPLE: A REPORT SUBMITTED TO THE SOUTHWEST COUNCIL OF LA RAZA, PHOENIX, ARIZONA. Albuquerque, N.Mex.: Southwestern Cooperative Educational Laboratory, 1969. iv, 110 p. Pap.

>   Dr. Valencia describes and evaluates the programs of sixteen ongoing projects (all except one in the Southwest) which he identified and visited in 1969. The programs deal with bilingual education, Spanish arts, teacher education, manpower, home education for underemployed seasonal agriculatural workers, youth motivation, and Head Start. Useful information is provided for those who are in the process of formulating, revising, and/or implementing new programs.

Sociology

CC-1 Bogardus, Emory Stephen. THE MEXICAN IN THE UNITED STATES. New York: Arno Press, 1970. 126 p. Biblio. Index. Tables.

>   Originally published in 1934. Intended as an objective study based on life histories, interviews, and psychosocial analyses of Mexican immigrants. Provides insights into the way of life of Mexican immigrants during the early 1930s. Includes an extensive annotated bibliography.

CC-2 Burma, John H. SPANISH-SPEAKING GROUPS IN THE UNITED STATES. Durham, N.C.: Duke University Press, 1954. ix, 214 p. Biblio. Maps.

>   The Spanish-speaking in this case are the Hispanos from New Mexico, Chicanos, and Mexicans as well as Filipinos and Puerto Ricans. The author studies the problems of assimilation encountered by these groups as they make their way in America's industrial centers.

CC-3 Carp, Frances M. FACTORS IN UTILIZATION OF SERVICES BY THE MEXICAN-AMERICAN ELDERLY. Palo Alto, Calif.: American Institute for Research, 1968. 117 p. Biblio. Tables. Pap.

The findings indicate that elderly Mexican Americans prefer to live in their own houses, poor as they may be, located near family members and friends, rather than move into public housing. It also became clear that they are not well informed with regard to public housing facilities or other services offered to the aged. Most information is obtained by word of mouth from kin or friends. The study was conducted with residents of San Antonio who were sixty-two years of age and older. These respondents were compared with Anglo-American respondents.

CC-4 Casavantes, Edward J. A NEW LOOK AT THE ATTRIBUTES OF THE MEXICAN AMERICAN. Albuquerque, N. Mex.: Southwestern Cooperative Educational Laboratory, 1969. N.p. [18]. Graphs. Refs. Tables. Pap.

The resurgence of ethnic pride among Chicanos has aroused interest in teaching Mexican American children something about their culture, but Casavantes finds there is no consensus about what should be taught in connection with cultural heritage. He notes that many characteristics of people living in the culture of poverty have been attributed to La Raza and agrees that they do apply, since a large percentage of this ethnic group lives in poverty. However, he does identify several distinctive characteristics, i.e., language, physical characteristics, religion, Mexican ancestry, which he labels as "structural-demographic attributes." He decries the damage done by stereotyping which comes from within the ethnic group as well as from outside.

CC-5 Farris, Buford E., and Hale, William M. MEXICAN-AMERICAN CONFLICT GANGS: OBSERVATIONS AND THEORETICAL IMPLICATIONS. Research and Educational Reports, no. 1. San Antonio, Tex.: Wesley Community Centers, 1962? 16 p. Biblio.

The authors attempt to examine the sociocultural and family forces which according to them seem to influence Chicano adolescents to participate collectively in violent actions. Unfortunately, the well-intentioned writers may have done more harm than good by drawing their assumptions from a rather superficial study. The authors are correct in acknowledging that their observations and assumptions require much more additional study and analysis.

CC-6 Galarza, Ernesto, et al. MEXICAN AMERICANS IN THE SOUTHWEST. Photos by George Ballis. Santa Barbara, Calif.: McNally and Loftin,

Publishers, 1969. xi, 90 p. App. B & w photos. Pap.

A report on what the authors saw and heard over a two-year period as they traveled in various parts of the United States and Mexico to observe and seek first-hand information about La Raza in its own setting. These words summarize their finds: "We saw poverty, hunger, despair and defeat. But we also saw hope in the eyes of many."

CC-7 Goldner, Norman. THE MEXICAN IN THE NORTHERN URBAN AREA: A COMPARISON OF TWO GENERATIONS. Dissertation, University of Minnesota, 1959. Reprint. San Francisco: R and E Research Associates, 1972. x, 123 p. Apps. Biblio. Tables. Pap.

Among the most prominent changes observed are that second generation Chicanos have acquired more education, have smaller families, attend church less frequently, have a better standard of living, hold higher level occupational positions, are more politically involved, and more assimilated into the American mainstream. By contrast the first generation retains much of its cultural identity, speaks more Spanish, does not aspire to managerial and professional-type employment positions, and is content with the status quo. Both generations show preference for Mexican-style food. In the appendices there is the schedule that was administered to fifty respondents and a list of the publications read by the respondents.

CC-8 Gomez, David F. SOMOS CHICANOS: STRANGERS IN OUR OWN LAND. Boston: Beacon Press, 1973. 233 p. Biblio. B & w photos. Gloss. Index.

In the brief autobiographical sketch which precedes the text, the reader learns that the author is an ex-priest who became incensed over the injustices imposed upon Mexican Americans and disenchanted with the Church's lack of response to the needs of the poor. Although the work is subjective, the author supports his reasoning with documentation as he narrates what it means to be a part of La Raza. Topics include education, poverty, the Church, and the Movimiento.

CC-9 Gutierrez, Jose Angel. A GRINGO MANUAL ON HOW TO HANDLE MEXICANS. Piedras Negras, Mexico: Imprenta Velasco Burckhardt, 1973? vii, 186 p. Pap.

The author explains 141 different "tricks" used by those in the power structure to render the Chicano powerless. One hundred and seventeen of the "movidas" are translated into Spanish. The tricks are divided into cate-

gories which vary from law and order to education and
employment. The writer hopes that Chicanos will employ this knowledge against the Gringo. Cleverly written, and at times tongue-in-cheek in style, but the
seriousness of the message never ceases to come through.

CC-10 Heller, Celia S. MEXICAN AMERICAN YOUTH: FORGOTTEN YOUTH
AT THE CROSSROADS. New York: Random House, 1966. vii, 113 p.
Biblio. Index. Tables. Pap.

The focus is on the male Chicano youth of Los Angeles.
More specifically, the "ambitious boys" as determined
by their upward mobility aspirations and the "delinquent
boys" as singled out by their pattern of offenses. Findings tend to indicate that the "ambitious" youths have
adopted the goals and values of the dominant society.
The "delinquents" are those who have had an unsatis-
factory school experience and suffer from low status.
They find solace in "gang" associations. One is left
with the impression that the conclusions need more in-
depth study. Delinquency among Chicanos has yet to
be considered in the total social and psychological environment involving culture conflict, poverty, and minority status.

CC-11 _____. NEW CONVERTS TO THE AMERICAN DREAM? MOBILITY
ASPIRATIONS OF YOUNG MEXICAN AMERICANS. New Haven,
Conn.: College & University Press, 1971. 287 p. Apps. Notes &
refs. Tables. Index.

This study suggests a trend toward upward mobility for
Mexican Americans. Its facts were ascertained by anal-
yzing the responses to a questionnaire administered to
seniors in ten high schools in the Los Angeles metropol-
itan area and the use of I.Q. scores as well as each
student's course of study. Excerpts from interviews with
eighteen mobility-oriented boys ranging from seventeen
to twenty years of age illustrate the findings.

CC-12 Madsen, William. MEXICAN-AMERICANS OF SOUTH TEXAS. New
York: Holt, Rinehart and Winston, 1964. 129 p. B & w photos. Map.
Recomd. read.

Based on research and ethnographic field work conducted
between 1957 and 1961, the author presents an anthropologist's concept of the sociocultural conditions of
Mexican Americans in Hidalgo County, Texas. Chicanos are viewed sympathetically and some educational
insights are provided, but the findings sketch over-sim-
plified situations which tend to draw stereotypes instead
of real people.

CC-13 Mangold, Margaret M., ed. LA CAUSA CHICANA: THE MOVEMENT FOR JUSTICE. Foreword by Juan Ramos. New York: Family Service Association of America, 1972. xiii, 218 p. Index.

> The principal target reader is the social worker. The purpose is to provide information which will lead to better understanding of Chicanos by those working with them. Twenty-nine (eight women) Mexican American writers cover such topics as the Chicano Movement, psychological research, religion, literature, social work, and the socioeconomic and cultural conditions of migrant workers. They have tried to demonstrate that effective service to Chicanos is not only up to individuals, but educational institutions and service agencies as well will need to remove barriers which obstruct the self-realization of those persons who have a different cultural and historical background.

CC-14 Minnesota. Governor's Interracial Commission. THE MEXICAN IN MINNESOTA. Rev. ed. Eighth of a series of reports to the Governor on various racial and religious situations which may affect the public welfare in Minnesota. 1953. Reprint. San Francisco: R and E Research Associates, 1972. 84 p. Pap.

> Five years after the first report was made, the new findings showed that the "Mexican" people were gradually being assimilated into Minnesota's population with relatively few problems. Then, too, mechanization of beet harvesting discouraged migrants from coming to this part of the country and those who already lived in the state preferred to work in industry. Since the Commission found this ethnic group to be making a worthwhile contribution to the state, various recommendations were made to attract and retain "Mexicans." The latter term is used in this report to designate persons of Indo-Hispanic ancestry, regardless of whether they were Mexican Americans or Mexican nationals.

CC-15 Mittelbach, Frank G., and Marshall, Grace. THE BURDEN OF POVERTY. Mexican-American Study Project. Advance Report, no. 5. Los Angeles: Division of Research, Graduate School of Business Administration, University of California, 1966. xi, 65 p. Apps. Chap. notes. Graphs. Tables. Pap.

> By comparing the incidence of poverty among Anglos, Chicanos, and nonwhites, the authors of this report have underscored the seriousness of the problem among Mexican Americans in the Southwest. Poverty among Spanish-surname families proves to be well over twice the Anglo rate. In the case of nonwhites it was two and one-half times the white Anglo rate. Information is also provided on those characteristics which account

for poverty; namely, farm employment, age, and broken
families. The closing chapter discusses the relationship
between family size and poverty. If poverty begets
poverty, as the researchers indicate, the two million
persons (Chicano and nonwhite) identified as being in
this state in 1960 have no doubt multiplied manyfold.

CC-16 Mittelbach, Frank G., et al. INTERMARRIAGE OF MEXICAN-AMERI-
CANS. Mexican-American Study Project. Advance Report, no. 6.
Los Angeles: Division of Research, Graduate School of Business Administration, University of California, 1966. vii, 84 p. Apps. Chap.
notes. Tables. Pap.

Analysis is based on "previous research on marriage in
stratified societies, both in the United States and in
other countries." Data pertinent to Mexican Americans
is derived primarily from marriage licenses issued in Los
Angeles County and San Antonio, Texas. Findings indicate that assimilation through intermarriage is still
not imminent as the majority of Chicanos still tend to
marry within their own ethnic group. Among those who
do marry out of the group are women, young rather
than older persons, and third-generation individuals.
Occupation, more than generation, is a determinant
in predicting who will marry out of the group. Finally,
there is more of a tendency among middle-class Mexican Americans to select spouses in terms of class rather
than ethnicity.

CC-17 Moore, Joan W., and Cuellar, Alfredo. MEXICAN AMERICANS. Englewood Cliffs, N.J.: Prentice-Hall, 1970. 188 p. Biblio. Index.
Graphs. Tables.

A profile of Mexican Americans in the Southwest based
on documented information. The authors first provide
historical background and then proceed to analyze the
socioeconomic forces which have shaped the lives of
the people who make up the second largest ethnic minority in the United States.

CC-18 Moore, Joan W., and Mittelbach, Frank G. RESIDENTIAL SEGREGA-
TION IN THE URBAN SOUTHWEST: A COMPARATIVE STUDY. Mexi-
can American Study Project. Advance Report, no. 4. Los Angeles:
Division of Research, Graduate School of Business Administration, Uni-
versity of California, 1966. 73 p. Apps. Chap. notes. Graphs.
Tables. Pap.

This study analyzed residential segregation patterns in
thirty-five cities on a comparative basis. The findings
showed Blacks to be victims of the most severe residential segregation by the dominant Anglo group. A high

degree of segregation also takes place between Blacks
and Chicanos. Chicanos are found to be substantially
less segregated from Anglos than Blacks, but the level
of segregation for both groups has remained high. Income differentials are factors related to residential segregation between Chicanos and Blacks. The less acculturated Mexican Americans are, the more likely they
are to share segregated areas with Blacks. The culture
factor plays an important part in the segregation of
Chicanos from Anglos, but is not a factor for Blacks
and Anglos. See also CG-24.

CC-19 Morefield, Richard. THE MEXICAN ADAPTATION IN AMERICAN
CALIFORNIA, 1846-1875. 1955. Reprint. San Francisco: R and E
Research Associates, 1971. vii, 106 p. App. Biblio. Tables.

Departing from the belief that closer attention should be
given to successful assimilation, the author examines
the "areas of group contact between the American and
the Mexicans in California in the first generation after
the area was ceded to the United States." This well-
intentioned study comes through as much too slanted.
The alert reader will recognize the omission of the
state's history of racial strife and violence even though
the author believes it has been overemphasized.

CC-20 Oxnam, Garfield Bromley. THE MEXICAN IN LOS ANGELES: LOS
ANGELES CITY SURVEY. Los Angeles: Interchurch World Movement of
North America. Reprint. San Francisco: R and E Research Associates,
1970. 28 p. Graphs. Maps. Pap.

Originally published in 1920. Although outdated and
generally superficial in content, this study provides information regarding such matters as housing, illiteracy,
health conditions, crime, employment, poverty, immigration, and emigration as they pertained to the Mexican American in Los Angeles. The advance work of
the Protestant Christian forces who were formulating
plans to attract the people of Mexican extraction.

CC-21 Penalosa, Fernando. CLASS CONSCIOUSNESS AND SOCIAL MOBILITY
IN A MEXICAN-AMERICAN COMMUNITY. Dissertation, University of
Southern California, 1963. Reprint. San Francisco: R and E Research
Associates, 1971. ix, 145 p. Apps. Biblio. Map. Tables. Pap.

Unlike other studies which have focused on barrios,
Penalosa's consisted of a cross-section (six percent area
sample or 147 adult persons) of the entire Mexican
American population of the city of Pomona, California,
in which he investigated social stratification and mobility.
Nearly two-fifths of the respondents used criteria of

economic position to describe class structure, while one-fifth used occupation. There was a high correlation between status index scores and schooling and education. The second generation was identified as the most upwardly mobile along with individuals who used English as opposed to Spanish, and who were in the younger age bracket.

CC-22 Peon, Maximo. COMO VIVEN LOS MEXICANOS EN LOS ESTADOS UNIDOS. Mexico: B. costa-Amic, 1966. 270 p.

An educated Mexican who worked for a relatively short period in various parts of the United States writes about his experiences and those of other braceros. The remarks concerning Mexican Americans are limited, but no less informative as they reflect a Mexican's point of view.

CC-23 Poggie, John J., Jr. BETWEEN TWO CULTURES: THE LIFE OF AN AMERICAN-MEXICAN AS TOLD TO JOHN J. POGGIE, JR. Tucson: University of Arizona Press, 1973. 108 p. Map.

Mexican-born Ramon Gonzalez grew up in the United States, but was deported because he never acquired U.S. citizenship. He kept coming back to the United States because his way of life was that of a Chicano. Finally, after being deported nine times, he resigned himself to living in Mexico permanently where he is considered a pocho.

CC-24 Rubel, Arthur J. ACROSS THE TRACKS: MEXICAN AMERICANS IN A TEXAS CITY. Austin: University of Texas Press for the Hogg Foundation for Mental Health, 1966. 266 p. Biblio. B & w photos. Gloss. Index. Tables.

Two years of anthropological research made it possible for the author to take a close look at the Chicano's way of life in a small city in the lower Rio Grande Valley. While the group continues to retain traditional cultural attitudes and behavior, it is caught between the conflicting goals and values of Anglo and Chicano cultures. There are problems yet to be overcome, among them those related to health.

CC-25 Ruiz, Juliette, ed. CHICANO TASK FORCE REPORT. New York: Council on Social Work Education, 1973. v, 24 p. App. Biblio. Pap.

As an outgrowth of the Council, the Task Force was charged with the responsibility of identifying "key problems and issues in the Chicano community as they re-

lated to social work education." A summary of those
issues and accompanying recommendations is the sub-
stance of the first half of the report. The second half
includes a prospectus for planning and implementation.

CC-26 Samora, Julian, and Lamanna, Richard A. MEXICAN AMERICANS IN
A MIDWEST METROPOLIS: A STUDY OF EAST CHICAGO. Mexican
American Study Project. Advance Report, no. 8. Los Angeles: Divi-
sion of Research, Graduate School of Business Administration, University
of California, 1967. x, 164 p. Apps. Chap. notes. Graphs. Maps.
Pap.

This study, which deals with the political and socioeconomic characteristics of Mexican Americans in East
Chicago, was conducted to determine, among other
reasons, whether this segment of the population differed
from the Chicanos in the Southwest. The study proved
that the industrial environment has had little, if any,
influence on its Mexican American community. Individual assimilation is occurring, but it is limited and takes
place slowly. Economically, Mexican Americans in
this area are among the poorest. Politically they are
powerless, though there are signs of improvement. In
education they are in a situation comparable to that of
their counterparts in the Southwest. As for social in-
tegration, ethnicity continues to play a vital role;
Chicanos remain Chicanos regardless of geographic location.

CC-27 Solis Garza, Hernan. LOS MEXICANOS DEL NORTE. Mexico City:
Editorial Nuestro Tiempo, 1971. 140 p.

A self-analysis by the author based on the writings of
such authors as Samuel Ramos and Octavio Paz. The
author describes Northern Mexicans from psychological,
sociological, anthropological, and historical viewpoints.
Since their life style, historical background, and culture
are intertwined with that of Mexican Americans in the
Southwest, the content of this work has relevance for
Chicanos.

CC-28 Tuck, Ruth D. NOT WITH THE FIST: MEXICAN AMERICANS IN A
SOUTHWEST CITY. New York: Harcourt, Brace and Co., 1946. 254
p. Biblio.

An attempt is made to describe the Chicano way of life
in a small, typical California city. The objective is
not quite fulfilled. Possibly because the author sees
Chicanos as the product of a standardized mold rather
than as individuals. Descanso is the fictitious and
symbolic name chosen for the city in the test tube.
Unfortunately, there is little rest in such communities,

particularly in the barrios. But the author has not failed completely. The Chicanos in Descanso who are groping to stay afloat in an industrial whirlpool that is fast swallowing up their traditional ways can also be found in similar cities throughout the Southwest. The book is intended for professionals working with La Raza. With an open mind, even Chicanos will find it worth reading.

CC-29 Upham, W. Kennedy, and Wright, David E. POVERTY AMONG SPAN-ISH AMERICANS IN TEXAS: LOW-INCOME FAMILIES IN A MINOR-ITY GROUP. College Station, Tex.: Department of Agricultural Economics and Sociology, Texas A & M University, 1966. 54 p. Maps. Tables.

Provides data on the economic and social characteristics of Mexican Americans of Texas with an annual family income of less than $3,000.

Anthropology

Bibliography

CD-1 Mickey, Barbara H. A BIBLIOGRAPHY OF STUDIES CONCERNING THE SPANISH-SPEAKING POPULATION OF THE AMERICAN SOUTH-WEST. Greeley: Colorado State College, Museum of Anthropology, 1969. 42 p. Pap.

Includes 544 entries, primarily concerned with anthropological studies of the Spanish-speaking people of the Southwest. Cites published and unpublished materials arranged in alphabetical order by author.

Anthropology

CD-2 Barker, George C. SOCIAL FUNCTIONS OF LANGUAGE IN A MEXI-CAN-AMERICAN COMMUNITY. Anthropological Papers of the University of Arizona, no. 22. Tucson: University of Arizona Press, 1972. iii, 56 p. Biblio. Pap.

Considering Spanish-speaking Mexican Americans residing in Tucson who are in the process of cultural change, the author in his study determined, among other findings, that Spanish is the language used for intimate and family relations. English is reserved for formal social relations and for communication with Anglos. Formal Spanish is used only by Mexican Americans who have a social relationship with Mexican nationals. Also, Mexican Americans who are interested in "making it" in Anglo society avoid the use of Spanish. People who

maintain an affiliation with Mexico prefer to converse
in Spanish with Anglos who know the language. A
third group, made up of young Chicanos, reject both
English and Spanish in favor of their own language--
Pachuco. This work originally constituted the author's
doctoral dissertation.

CD-3 Goldstein, Marcus S. DEMOGRAPHIC AND BODILY CHANGES IN
DESCENDENTS OF MEXICAN IMMIGRANTS, WITH COMPARABLE DATA
ON PARENTS AND CHILDREN IN MEXICO. Austin: Institute of Latin-
American Studies, University of Texas, 1943. 103 p. Apps. Pap.

In ascertaining the biological effects of environment,
176 Mexican immigrant families (mostly from San Antonio), including their first generation American-born
children were examined in Texas. The control group
consisted of 129 families examined in Mexico. The
findings showed appreciable changes between the immigrants and their adult children. However, the same
changes were also found in the children of Mexican
nationals, but not to the same degree. One notable
change showed a greater increase in stature for the
American-born offspring. Results also showed the Mexican mestizo to be somewhat taller than the Spaniard.

CD-4 Helm, June, ed. SPANISH-SPEAKING PEOPLE IN THE UNITED STATES.
PROCEEDINGS OF THE 1968 ANNUAL SPRING MEETING OF THE
AMERICAN ETHNOLOGICAL SOCIETY. Seattle: University of Wash-
ington Press, 1968. vi, 215 p. Graphs. Refs. Tables.

As the title suggests, the content consists of papers prepared by specialists. Most are concerned with Mexican
Americans, although there is one on Spanish-speaking
people in Florida which deals with Puerto Ricans and
Cubans as well as Chicanos. There is also one on the
Blackfoot Indian which appears to be out place. Among
the topics relating to Chicanos are generalizations made
by anthropologists regarding cultural attributes, assimilation and acculturation, life in an urban barrio, folk
medicine, and the Alianza Movement as a catalyst for
social change in New Mexico.

CD-5 Kiev, Ari. CURANDERISMO: MEXICAN-AMERICAN FOLK PSYCHIA-
TRY. New York: The Free Press, 1968. 220 p. Biblio. Index.

Dr. Kiev, who has compiled an anthology of writings
dealing with prescientific psychiatric theories and practices of several cultures throughout the world, in this
book examines the role of the curandero operating in
his own culture and his effectiveness in dealing with
the psychopathological afflictions of his patients. He

finds that the <u>curandero</u> can be more effective with certain patients requiring psychotherapy than scientifically trained doctors. This work is based primarily on interviews with four Texas <u>curanderos</u>, as well as the researcher's study of patients suffering psychiatric illness and the experience gained by treating Chicano patients with conventional psychotherapeutic methods.

CD-6 Swadesh, Frances Leon. HISPANIC AMERICANS OF THE UTE FRONTIER FROM THE CHAMA VALLEY TO THE SAN JUAN BASIN, 1694-1960. Tri-ethnic Research Project Research Report, no. 50. Boulder: University of Colorado, 1966. 325 p. Biblio.

Through archival research and fieldwork, the author "attempts to apply the methods of structural analysis to sets of data in historical perspective, such prevailing patterns of community settlement, of residential grouping and of household composition.... This study assembles data to indicate that comparable adaptive vitality may be latent in this <u>Hispano</u> population of northern New Mexico and southwestern Colorado."

Folklore & Popular Customs

Bibliography

CE-1 Tully, Marjorie F., and Rael, Juan B., comps. AN ANNOTATED BIBLIOGRAPHY OF SPANISH FOLKLORE IN NEW MEXICO AND SOUTHERN COLORADO. University of New Mexico Publications in Language and Literature, no. 3. Albuquerque: University of New Mexico Press, 1950. 124 p. Subject index.

Originally begun as Miss Tully's master's thesis and later revised and enlarged by Professor Rael. Intended as a guide to the literature in the subject. It contains book titles, periodical articles, and book reviews. Although limited primarily to books and periodicals examined by the compilers at the libraries of Stanford University and the University of California at Berkeley, a few manuscripts listed in Lyle Saunders' A GUIDE TO MATERIALS BEARING ON CULTURAL RELATIONS IN NEW MEXICO (see AA-6) are also included. Entries are arranged alphabetically by author. Annotations are descriptive, uncritical, and generally very brief.

Folklore & Popular Customs

CE-2 Campa, Arthur Leon. SPANISH FOLK-POETRY IN NEW MEXICO. Albuquerque: University of New Mexico Press, 1946. 224 p. Biblio.

The content is devoted mostly to representative songs
sung by the Spanish-speaking folk people of New Mexico. An informative introduction deals with the history
of New Mexico and its Spanish-speaking population.
The songs included are classified under romances, corridos, decimas, and canciones.

CE-3 _____ . TREASURE OF THE SANGRE DE CRISTOS; TALES AND TRA-
DITIONS OF THE SPANISH SOUTHWEST. Illustrated by Joe Beeler.
Norman: University of Oklahoma Press, 1963. 238 p. Biblio. B &
w draws. Index. Map.

The author, a well-known folklorist, relates tales,
legends, and anecdotes which he has collected over
many years. Some of this folklore is the traditional
heritage of his family, another part was acquired during
his childhood days when he lived on a Texas rancho,
and still another part was contributed by old timers and
other persons who altogether have helped to assemble
a series of entertaining stories. The more frequent subjects are lost mines, buried treasure, old landmarks, and
the Indians and Spaniards.

CE-4 _____ , comp. "Spanish Religious Folktheatre in the Spanish Southwest
(First Cycle)." UNIVERSITY OF NEW MEXICO BULLETIN, Language
Series, vol. 5, no. 1, February 15, 1934. Albuquerque: University of
New Mexico Press, 1934. 71 p. Biblio.

The author finds that there are two cycles of religious
plays. The first deals with Biblical subjects of the Old
Testament. The second originates with the marriage of
Joseph and Mary and ends with the journey to Bethlehem
(see CE-5). This volume includes two plays of the first
cycle: "Adam and Eve" and "Cain and Abel."

CE-5 _____ , comp. "Spanish Religious Folktheatre in the Southwest (Second
Cycle)." UNIVERSITY OF NEW MEXICO BULLETIN, Language Series,
vol. 5, no. 2, June 15, 1934. Albuquerque: University of New Mexico Press, 1934. 157 p. Biblio.

Included in this volume are the following plays representative of the second cycle: "Coloquio de San Jose,"
"Coloquio de Pastores," "Auto de Los Reyes Magos,"
and "El Nino Perdido." See also CE-4.

CE-6 Espinosa, Aurelio Macedonio. ROMANCERO DE NUEVO MEJICO. Revista de Filologia Espanola, anjeo 58. Madrid: Instituto Miguel de Cer-
vantes, Consejo Superior de Investigaciones Cientificas, 1953. 302 p.
Biblio.

Probably the largest and one of the more important col-

lections of ballads gathered in New Mexico. Contains
248 versions of ninety different ballads. Among them
are corridos, cuandos, inditas, alabados, and alabanzas.
Of the ninety different compositions, twenty-one are
classified as traditional romances, sixteen are novelistic-
type ballads presented in eighty-nine versions, and eleven are religious ballads in fifty-six versions. The text
is supplemented with the list of narrators and a section
of musical scores for twenty-eight of the ballads, traditional and popular.

CE-7 Espinosa, Jose Manuel. SPANISH FOLK-TALES FROM NEW MEXICO.
New York: The American Folklore Society, G.E. Stechert and Co.,
agents, 1937. 241 p. Biblio. Notes. Gloss.

Included are 114 folktales gathered from seven counties--
Taos, Santa Fe, Rio Arriba, Sandoval, Bernalillo, Valencia, and Guadalupe--located in the north and central
part of New Mexico. These tales were transcribed by
the compiler directly from the mouths of the Spanish-
speaking narrators. The tales are divided into the following six groupings: magic tales, religious tales, picaresque tales, romantic tales, short tales and anecdotes,
and animal tales. English summaries are provided.

CE-8 Jaramillo, Cleofas M. SHADOWS OF THE PAST (SOMBRAS DEL PASA-
DO). Illustrated by author. Santa Fe, N. Mex.: Seton Village Press,
1941. 116 p.

The author, a descendent of a prominent New Mexican
pioneer family, writes about customs, habits, beliefs,
and the folklore which she recalls from an era that represents the Hispanos' old way of life. The Spanish
words and phrases interjected in her prose give distinct
flavor and authenticity to descriptive passages on folk
art, games and sports, and religious customs and dramas
of her day. Altogether one senses the author's deeply-
felt appreciation for her Hispanic heritage. Some poetry,
games, songs, and alabados are included.

CE-9 Martinez, Rafael V. MY HOUSE IS YOUR HOUSE. New York: Friend-
ship Press, 1964. 127 p. B & w illus. & ports.

The author provides insights into the Hispanic heritage
and brings out the cultural contributions made to the
United States by Cubans, Puerto Ricans, Mexican Americans, and other Spanish-speaking peoples. Emphasis is
on music, dance, and the other performing arts.

CE-10 Miller, Elaine K., comp. MEXICAN FOLK NARRATIVE FROM THE
LOS ANGELES AREA. Publications of the American Folklore Society.

Memoir Series, vol. 56. Introduction, notes, and classification by Elaine K. Miller. Austin: Published for the American Folklore Society by the University of Texas Press, 1973. 388 p. Biblio. Indexes. B & w photos.

The author's revised doctoral dissertation serves as the content of this work which includes eighty-two narratives collected from twenty-seven informants in Los Angeles and environs, e.g., Santa Paula, Oxnard, Culver City, Santa Monica, Venice, and West Los Angeles. The narratives are classified and documented according to accepted standard reference works. Unfortunately, for the most part old-time California, Spanish-speaking residents were bypassed. The three appendixes provide: index of tale types, motifs index, and glossary.

CE-11 Paredes, Americo. "WITH HIS PISTOL IN HIS HANDS," A BORDER BALLAD AND ITS HERO. Austin: University of Texas Press, 1958. 262 p. Biblio. Illus.

A study of the Texas ballad entitled, "El Corrido de Gregorio Cortez." Provides a factual account of this ballad hero and the way in which songs and folk traditions have developed about him.

CE-12 Rael, Juan Bautista, ed. CUENTOS ESPANOLES DE COLORADO Y NUEVO MEJICO. SPANISH TALES FROM COLORADO AND NEW MEXICO; SPANISH ORIGINALS WITH ENGLISH SUMMARIES. 2 vols. Stanford, Calif.: Stanford University Press, 1957. Biblio. Pap. Append.

In the foreword the late renowned New Mexican folklorist, Professor Aurelio M. Espinosa, described this work as "... easily the best and most abundant collection of folktales that we now have from Spanish America." The collection consists of a total of 518 stories, most of which were transcribed as narrated by folk people of the Spanish-speaking communities in New Mexico. The text is arranged under these categories: tales of riddles, tales of human beings, moral tales, enchantment tales, picaresque tales, and animal tales. The appendix includes additional tales collected ten years after the original collection was compiled in 1930, together with the English summaries.

CE-13 Robe, Stanley L., ed. ANTOLOGIA DEL SABER POPULAR: A SELECTION FROM VARIOUS GENRES OF MEXICAN FOLKLORE ACROSS BORDERS. Chicano Studies Center Monograph, no. 2. Los Angeles: Aztlan Publications, University of California, 1971. 93 p. Pap.

The selected writings show that there are no political boundaries for folklore. Consequently, much of the

Chicano folklore originated in Mexico. Samples of various types are represented in this work--folktales, jests, anecdotes, legends, beliefs, prayers, children's games, lullabies, and riddles. Corridos are not included because it was felt that justice could not be done to them without their accompanying music. The contributors are students of Mexican background enrolled at the University of California at Los Angeles. Most of the material included was obtained from informants in the Los Angeles area with some contributions by individuals from Arizona and Texas.

CE-14 Simmons, Marc. WITCHCRAFT IN THE SOUTHWEST: SPANISH AND INDIAN SUPERNATURALISM ON THE RIO GRANDE. Flagstaff, Ariz.: Northland Press, 1974. xiii, 184 p. Biblio. Notes. B & w photos.

A professional historian presents a documented overview of the history and practice of witchcraft among the Spanish-speaking population and the communal Indians of the Rio Grande region which extends from the Texas gulf coast to southern Colorado. The reading proves fascinating and informative, particularly since brujas, hechiceria, curanderas, and the use of hierbas remain very much alive today among the economically disadvantaged Mexican Americans and Indians. The writer concludes by saying, "...who at present is so well versed in all things that he can pretend to know the extent of the power of belief."

CE-15 Waugh, Julia Nott. THE SILVER CRADLE. Drawings by Bob Winn. Austin: University of Texas Press, 1955. 160 p.

The author, who describes herself as not Mexican, Catholic, nor scholar, writes about the manner in which poor Mexican Americans of San Antonio celebrate Christmas, Easter and Epiphany, Mexican Independence Day, the blessing of animals, and the greeting of the Virgin of Guadalupe.

Statistics

CF-1 Browning, Harley L., and McLemore, S. Dale. A STATISTICAL PROFILE OF THE SPANISH-SURNAME POPULATION OF TEXAS. Austin: Bureau of Business Research, University of Texas, 1964. 83 p. Maps. Tables. Pap.

The data were taken from two reports published in 1950 (see CF-6) and 1960 by the Bureau of the Census under the title PERSONS OF SPANISH SURNAME, as well as from other census sources. The report does not propose to give an

exact count nor to explain the statistics. It identifies
the main features and characteristics of the Spanish-
surnamed population and compares them with those of
the Anglo and nonwhite. The basic characteristics
looked at include size and distribution of the population, age and sex composition, fertility and mortality
rates, educational attainment, employment by occupation and industry, and individual and family income.

CF-2 California. Department of Industrial Relations. CALIFORNIANS OF
SPANISH SURNAME. 1964. Reprint. San Francisco: Fair Employment Practice Commission, Division of Fair Employment Practices, 1969.
54 p. Tables. Pap.

The intent of this report is to encourage governmental
agencies at all levels as well as educational institutions
to find and implement solutions to problems which have
made Spanish-speaking Californians victims of discrimination and unemployment because of differences in culture, language, and educational handicaps. Most of
the information is statistical and taken from the 1960
CENSUS OF POPULATION. It deals with the person's
place of birth and residence, education, employment,
unemployment, and income.

CF-3 California. Mexican Fact-Finding Committee. MEXICANS IN CALIF-
ORNIA: REPORT OF GOVERNOR C.C. YOUNG'S MEXICAN FACT-.
FINDING COMMITTEE, 1930. Reprint. San Francisco: R and E
Research Associates, 1970. 214 p. Graphs. Maps. Tables. Pap.

Prepared to show the actual existing conditions of the
"Mexican" population in the state, the report is divided into four parts and deals specifically with these
topics: (1) immigration, population, and naturalization;
(2) employment in industry and nonagricultural occupa-
tions; (3) needs of manual labor and its effect upon
agriculture; (4) health, relief, and delinquency conditions. Most of the data for (4) pertains to Los Angeles
County. Although the work is dated, its statistical information, in particular, is of historical value.

CF-4 Fellows, Lloyd. ECONOMIC ASPECTS OF THE MEXICAN RURAL POP-
ULATION IN CALIFORNIA WITH SPECIAL EMPHASIS ON THE NEED
FOR MEXICAN LABOR IN AGRICULTURE (1929). Reprint. San Fran-
cisco: R and E Research Associates, 1971. iii, 95 p. App. Biblio.
Tables. Pap.

A statistical study based on the results of a number of
surveys made in Mexico and California. The object of
the study was to show a relationship between Mexican
immigration and the need for farm labor from Mexico in
California.

CF-5   Talbert, Robert Harris. SPANISH NAME PEOPLE IN THE SOUTHWEST
       AND WEST: SOCIOECONOMIC CHARACTERISTICS OF WHITE PERSONS
       OF SPANISH SURNAME IN TEXAS, ARIZONA, CALIFORNIA, COLO-
       RADO, AND NEW MEXICO. Fort Worth, Tex.: Leo Potishman Foun-
       dation, Texas Christian University, 1955. 90 p. Biblio. Index. Tables.

       An attempt to present in usable form selected statistical
       information from the 1950 U.S. Census of Population
       and Housing concerning education, marital and econo-
       mic status, and housing.

CF-6   U.S. Bureau of the Census. Census of Population: 1970. Subject Re-
       ports. PERSONS OF SPANISH SURNAME. Washington, D.C.: Gover-
       ment Printing Office, 1973. vii, 146 p. Apps. Tables.

       Provides social, economic, and housing data for persons
       of Spanish surname in Arizona, California, Colorado,
       New Mexico, and Texas. Specific information includes
       educational attainment, earnings, employment status,
       class of worker, and income per person in 1969. Hous-
       ing data includes the number of persons per room, units
       in structure, year structure was built, value, and con-
       tract rent. Information on poverty status and available
       automobiles also listed. Five appendices provide defi-
       nitions, sources of error in data, and other explanatory
       information.

Economics & Labor

Bibliography

CG-1   Institute for Rural America. POVERTY, RURAL POVERTY AND MINOR-
       ITY GROUPS LIVING IN RURAL POVERTY: AN ANNOTATED BIBLI-
       OGRAPHY. Lexington, Ky.: Spindletop Research, 1969. 159 p.

       Selective unnotated resource surveys social, economic,
       and demographic characteristics, discrimination, labor
       patterns, legislation, and land reform concerning Mexi-
       can Americans in rural poverty. Titles are arranged by
       subject.

CG-2   U.S. Department of Agriculture. RESEARCH DATA ON MINORITY
       GROUPS: AN ANNOTATED BIBLIOGRAPHY OF ECONOMIC RESEARCH
       SERVICE REPORTS, 1955-1965. Washington, D.C.: Government Printing
       Office, 1966. 25 p. Pap.

       A few references to Mexican Americans are included
       among the low-income, rural minorities listed. Refer-
       ences are grouped according to geographic area, and
       alphabetically by author. Entries of monographs, arti-
       cles, and papers are followed by brief annotations. In-

dexed by author and subject.

CG-3 U.S. Department of Labor. SELECTED REFERENCES ON DOMESTIC MIGRATORY AGRICULTURAL WORKERS, THEIR FAMILIES, PROBLEMS, AND PROGRAMS, 1955-1960. Washington, D.C.: Government Printing Office, 1961. 38 p. Pap.

Includes materials from both governmental and nongovernmental sources dating from 1955 to mid-1960. Entries listed under subject, then arranged alphabetically by author. Annotations, prices, and availability are sometimes given.

CG-4 WEDCO: A BIBLIOGRAPHY. MATERIALS RELATING TO THE PROBLEMS OF THE MEXICO-UNITED STATES BORDER. Oakland, Calif.: The Western Economic Development Corporation, 1974. 29 p. Pap.

Compiled by a minority-owned and operated nonprofit firm, this bibliography should prove useful to those interested in studying the problem of alien workers as it affects the welfare of Chicanos. The entries are divided into ten topics which deal with matters such as the relations between the United States and Mexico, labor importation programs, illegal immigration, and Mexican migrant workers. The materials cited include books, periodical articles, a few theses, and a section devoted to government publications.

Biography

CG-5 Matthiessen, Peter. SAL SI PUEDES: CESAR CHAVEZ AND THE NEW AMERICAN REVOLUTION. New York: Random House, 1969. 372 p.

More than a biography of Chavez, it is a historical account of how the seasonal field workers of Kern County struggled to organize under the leadership of a man described both as a gentle mystic and a tough labor leader, singleminded to the point of ruthlessness.

Economics & Labor

CG-6 Allen, Steve. THE GROUND IS OUR TABLE. Photos by Arthur Dubinsky. Garden City, N.Y.: Doubleday, 1966. 141 p. B & w photos.

The author admits he wrote this book in anger, but makes no apologies. In straightforward language he discusses the plight of the farmworkers in the Southwest--most of whom are Mexican Americans. He points the finger at the strong, agricultural-business combines as being responsible for the existence and perpetuation of this socioeconomic dilemma. A chapter is devoted to the Delano strike.

CG-7 Baker, Bonnie Lea, et al. ECONOMIC ASPECTS OF MEXICAN AND MEXICAN-AMERICAN URBAN HOUSEHOLDS/ASPECTOS ECONOMICOS DE LA VIDA URBANA MEXICANA Y MEXICANA-AMERICANA: EL ENGANCHE ENTRE DOS MUNDOS. San Jose, Calif.: Institute for Business and Economic Research, San Jose State College, 1971. 150 p. App. Biblio. Graphs. Tables. Pap.

In comparing the buying habits of middle-class Mexicans living in Mexico City with those of Mexican Americans from San Jose, California, this bilingual study offers little comparative information in regard to economic behavior due to cultural factors. It does single out some differences on matters such as income, mobility, and property ownership. Whether an accurate comparative assessment between these two groups can be made is doubtful. One conclusion that does surface is that the cultural heritage of the Chicano does affect his economic behavior in terms of his family outlook, concept of time, and goals.

CG-8 BASTA! LA HISTORIA DE NUESTRA LUCHA. ENOUGH! THE TALE OF OUR STRUGGLE. Photos by George Ballis. Text from the Plan of Delano. Delano, Calif.: Farm Worker Press, 1966. 72 p. B & w photos.

"The faces and words that you see...will give you an idea of where we have been and a glimpse of where we are going." So said Cesar Chavez in the brief introduction of this public awareness pamphlet. There is little text, but what there is appears both in English and Spanish. The epic of the Delano farm workers is depicted largely through photos.

CG-9 Blair, Philip M. JOB DISCRIMINATION AND EDUCATION: AN INVESTMENT ANALYSIS. A CASE STUDY OF MEXICAN-AMERICANS IN SANTA CLARA COUNTY, CALIFORNIA. New York: Praeger Publishers, 1972. 269 p. Apps. Biblio. Tables.

Will an increased education place more money in the pocketbook of a Chicano? A total of 160,000 employed Chicano and Anglo male heads of households were studied in Santa Clara County. According to the findings the highest rate of economic return to Chicanos is reached at grade 10 1/2. The author states that "the greatest explainer of low Mexican-American return to diploma must be employment discrimination." Findings also showed that Chicano incomes over the entire schooling range were up to twenty percent smaller than the Anglo

income range. It was further determined that in 1966 the
unemployment rate for Chicanos was twelve percent as
compared with four percent for Anglos. A well-documented study which provides much food for thought on
the economics of education.

CG-10 Briggs, Vernon M., Jr. CHICANOS AND RURAL POVERTY. Policy
Studies in Employement & Welfare, no. 16. Baltimore: John Hopkins
University Press, 1973. 81 p. Tables.

Singles out and documents the principal issues involved
in the plight of rural Chicanos in the Southwest. It
shows how long years of back-breaking work have not
improved the socioeconomic conditions of farm workers
because these people have been caught in one of the
most exploitive industries in the nation.

CG-11 California. University. Heller Committee for Research in Social Economics and Panunzio, Constantine. COST OF LIVING STUDIES. V. HOW
MEXICANS EARN AND LIVE: A STUDY OF THE INCOMES AND EX-
PENDITURES OF ONE HUNDRED MEXICAN FAMILIES IN SAN DIEGO,
CALIFORNIA. University of California Publications in Economics, vol.
13, no. 1. Berkeley: University of California Press, 1933. ix, 114
p. Apps. Tables. Pap.

An outdated, but interesting study of one hundred "typical" families (parents were native Mexicans with three
or four children born in California; in each, the farmer
earned about $1000 a year as a low-skilled or semi-
skilled laborer) from San Diego who were studied to
determine their habits of living with a larger income
while in the process of acculturation. The findings
show that with the exception of retaining their food
habits, these families adopted American ways in cloth-
ing and housing.

CG-12 Copp, Nelson Gage. "WETBACKS" AND BRACEROS: MEXICAN MI-
GRANT LABORERS AND AMERICAN IMMIGRATION POLICY, 1930-1960.
Dissertation, Boston University Graduate School, 1963. Reprint. San
Francisco: R and E Research Associates, 1971. xi, 123 p. Apps.
Biblio. Tables. Pap.

This thirty-year survey tells the history of legal and illegal workmen from Mexico, the treaties between the
United States and Mexico dealing with Mexican laborers, and describes the problems which these persons en-
counter in this country. The author also discusses the
economic and immigration policies concerned with the
"wetback-bracero story." The appendices contain information on the number of Mexican nationals admitted
to the United States by decades. Information gathered

from interviews includes the number of times the laborers had entered the United States, how and why they had come, and what they planned to do with the money they earned.

CG-13 Day, Mark. FORTY ACRES: CESAR CHAVEZ AND THE FARM WORK-ERS. Introduction by Cesar Chavez. New York: Praeger Publishers, 1971. 222 p. App. Biblio. B & w photos.

Father Day, a young Catholic priest who joined the farm workers' movement in 1967, writes sympathetically about their struggles against the powerful California agricultural-business corporations. Another important part of this book are his observations in regard to the involvement or noninvolvement of the Church in the fight for social justice. "Forty Acres" is the place in Delano where Chavez fasted for twenty-five days and which later became the site for the United Farm Workers Organizing Committee's (UFWOC) headquarters.

CG-14 de Toledano, Ralph. LITTLE CESAR. Foreword by U.S. Senator Paul J. Fannin. Washington, D.C.: Anthem Books, 1971. 144 p. Pap.

The author, identified as a correspondent, columnist, and friend of former President Nixon, is no sympathizer of Cesar Chavez as the title of the book suggests. Supposedly this is the "true story of Delano and its grape pickers." Unfortunately, it turns out to be a biased interpretation and a distortion of facts. Needless to say, organized labor is taken to task.

CG-15 Dunne, John G. DELANO. Rev. ed. Photos by Ted Streshinsky. New York: Farrar, Straus & Giroux, 1971. 202 p. B & w photos.

Whereas in the first edition the narrative of the grape strike ended with the DiGiorgio Corp. agreeing to a contract, this revised version includes an assessment of the victory and a portrayal of Cesar Chavez. The simple, yet forceful style makes the book a good source of information on the subject for students and the layman.

CG-16 Fogel, Walter. MEXICAN AMERICANS IN SOUTHWEST LABOR MAR-KETS. Mexican American Study Project. Advance Report, no. 10. Los Angeles: Division of Research, Graduate School of Business Administration, University of California, 1967. ix, 222 p. Apps. Chap. notes. Tables. Pap.

In this comprehensive study the attention is on males, urban experiences, and the states of California and Texas. This orientation is explained on the basis of numbers. For example, there are far more men in the labor

force than women. The findings substantiate that Mexican Americans are definitely a disadvantaged group in
the Southwest labor markets. Reasons cited are low job
qualifications, low level of educational attainment, and
discrimination. Source of data is primarily the 1960 U.
S. CENSUS OF POPULATION.

CG-17 Galarza, Ernesto. SPIDERS IN THE HOUSE AND WORKERS IN THE
FIELD. Notre Dame: University of Notre Dame Press, 1970. 320 p.
Biblio.

Shows how the "establishment" as represented by the
courts and committees of the Congress have at times
contributed to the plight of impoverished Mexican American farm workers in California. The story of how things
were prior to Cesar Chavez.

CG-18 Harward, Naomi. SOCIO-ECONOMIC AND OTHER VARIATIONS RE-
LATED TO REHABILITATION OF MEXICAN AMERICANS IN ARIZONA.
FINAL REPORT OF A STUDY SUPPORTED IN PART BY...DEPARTMENT
OF HEALTH, EDUCATION, AND WELFARE, WASHINGTON, D.C.
Tempe: Bureau of Publications, Arizona State University, 1969. viii,
90 p. Biblio. Pap.

Primarily to analyze the effectiveness of vocational rehabilitation services to Chicanos, 150 members of this
ethnic group were equally matched with an Anglo control group and interviewed in regard to attitudes and
factors related to the rehabilitation process, i.e., attitude toward change, work, difficulty, dependency,
formal organization, and differences in language. The
findings showed no significant differences between the
two groups, contrary to what had previously been speci-
fied as typical for the Colorado and New Mexico Chicanos. The one major change noted was an increased
interest on the part of Chicanos to use Spanish as an
asset on their jobs. It was also determined that full-
time employment is of importance to most rehabilitants,
but whether their increased income would meet their
needs was not indicated. Job satisfaction is a factor
to consider in the total adjustment of these individuals,
but dissatisfaction with the job may also suggest inadequacy of wages and the rehabilitant's feelings about his
status.

CG-19 Horwitz, George D., and Fusco, Paul. LA CAUSA: THE CALIFORNIA
GRAPE STRIKE. Introduction by Cesar Chavez. New York: Macmillan,
1970. 158 p. B & w photos.

A writer and a photographer collaborate to depict the
movement that led to the organization of the now-famous

huelga against the Delano, California, grape workers.
The text, while interesting, is brief and lacks both
depth and breadth. The chief value of this work lies
in its photographs which dramatically convey the drab-
ness of poverty and its victims.

CG-20 Jones, Lamar Babington. MEXICAN-AMERICAN LABOR PROBLEMS IN
TEXAS. Dissertation, University of Texas at Austin, 1965. Reprint.
San Francisco: R and E Research Associates, 1971. vii, 127 p. Apps.
Biblio. Pap.

The demands of the United States employers for cheap
labor and Mexico's economic conditions have jointly
created and perpetuated a serious labor problem which
affects Chicano farm workers who are generally poor,
and lacking in education and skills. The subject is
timely and well-researched. Here the author "charts
the course national manpower policy has taken among
Mexican-American workers in the Texas border area."
He advocates "an end to the subsidization of economic
progress for Mexico and United States businesses at the
expense of generations of poverty for American citizens."
Most of the appendix is devoted to tables which record
data pertinent to the wage structure of various industries
in Laredo.

CG-21 Knox, William John. THE ECONOMIC STATUS OF THE MEXICAN
IMMIGRANT IN SAN ANTONIO, TEXAS. Thesis, University of Texas,
1927. Reprint. San Francisco: R and E Research Associates, 1971.
iii, 39 p. Tables. Pap.

Based on a survey conducted in 1925 of 1,440 families
(9,000 persons) or about one-eighth of the entire "Mexican" population of San Antonio, the author observes,
among other findings, that the majority had less than
four years of schooling and worked as unskilled migrant
workers. They showed "little evidence of improvement
toward a more skilled type" of work, and there was no
"tendency for Mexicans to affiliate with American labor." Their earning capacity was influenced by the
language barrier and limited schooling. The study is
superficial, but the data provided can be useful for
comparative purposes.

CG-22 Kostyu, Frank A. SHADOWS IN THE VALLEY: THE STORY OF ONE
MAN'S STRUGGLE FOR JUSTICE. Garden City, N.Y.: Doubleday &
Co., 1970. 192 p.

A Gringo minister, inspired by the work of Cesar Chavez
in California, joins the field workers in the Rio Grande
Valley in their struggle against the agri-business combines. Ed Krueger's confrontation with the Texas Ran-

gers, the law enforcement body with a long history for discriminatory treatment against Mexican Americans, contributes to his getting fired by the Texas Council of Churches, the organization that originally employed him to work with migrant workers. The reader is left, however, with the thought that because of the successful work of this determined minister and the support gained from Chicanos, the Valley will never be the same again.

CG-23 London, Joan, and Anderson, Henry. SO SHALL YE REAP. New York: Thomas Y. Crowell Co., 1970. xi, 208 p. B & w photos. Index. Map. Sugg. read.

Concerns the precursors of the farm workers' union in California and their long struggle to organize. Among the trailblazers discussed are Fathers Thomas McCullough and Donald McDonell, Fred Van Dyke, and Ernesto Galarza, with a few references to Delores Huerta. They are described as "profiles in failure," but without their contribution the movement would not have gained the success that it achieved (the manuscript was completed right after the Delano grape strike and boycott). Since a book on this topic could hardly be written without information on Cesar Chavez and his organizing methods, the last two chapters are devoted to him. The authors suggest that other sources be consulted for information on seasonal farm laborers because they are not the principal subject of this account.

CG-24 Moore, Joan W. MEXICAN-AMERICANS: PROBLEMS AND PROSPECTS. Madison: Institute for Research on Poverty, University of Wisconsin, 1966. 58 p. Graphs. Tables. Pap.

Prepared originally for the Office of Economic Opportunity, this study provides concise, researched background information which can be used as a source for policy-making relevant to Mexican Americans in the Southwest. The statistical information is now outdated, but there is still useful information on population, education, employment, and urban problems. Includes materials from the University of California Mexican American Study Project. See also CC-18.

CG-25 Moore, Truman. THE SLAVES WE RENT. Photos by author. New York: Random House, 1965. 171 p. Biblio. B & w photos. Index. Read. notes.

Deals broadly with migratory labor in the United States with only a small part specifically devoted to Mexican American seasonal farm workers. Yet the reader who wishes to become informed on this serious problem, which

afflicts a large percentage of the poor Chicano population, will profit from this knowledgeably written account.
The author believes that the migrant today is as out of
place in modern America as would be a slave ship in
New York harbor. Nevertheless, he sees seasonal labor
as an integral part of the "brave new farm" of the future.

CG-26 Nelson, Eugene. HUELGA: THE FIRST HUNDRED DAYS OF THE GREAT
DELANO GRAPE STRIKE. Delano, Calif.: Farm Worker Press, 1966.
127 p. B & w photos.

A former picket captain in the Delano grape strike presents an insider's viewpoint on the struggle of the poverty laboring population, mostly Chicano and Filipino-
American migrant workers, against the powerful corporations in the California agricultural-business. One chapter gives biographical information on Cesar Chavez.

CG-27 Schmidt, Fred H. SPANISH SURNAMED AMERICAN EMPLOYMENT IN
THE SOUTHWEST: A STUDY PREPARED FOR THE COLORADO CIVIL
RIGHTS COMMISSION UNDER THE AUSPICES OF THE EQUAL EMPLOY-
MENT OPPORTUNITY COMMISSION. Washington, D.C.: Government
Printing Office, 1970. v, 247 p. Apps. Graphs. Tables. Pap.

Using Bureau of the Census data from 1940 to 1966 and
employer reports, this documented inquiry concerned with
Southwest employment patterns has established that numbers have not made it any easier for Mexican Americans
to gain white-collar positions. Employment of Chicanos
in service, laborer, and operative jobs is far in excess
of its share in the labor force. In essence, the long
history of racial prejudice in this country has had a
lasting effect on the lives of Indians, Spanish-speaking,
Orientals, and Blacks. Problems for Chicanos are exa-
cerbated by immigration, contracting, and commuting of
workers from Mexico.

CG-28 Stambaugh, J. Lee, and Stambaugh, Lillian J. THE LOWER RIO
GRANDE VALLEY OF TEXAS. San Antonio: Naylor Co., 1954. 447
p. Biblio. B & w photos. Index. Maps. Tables.

Deals with the four Texas counties of Cameron, Hidalgo,
Starr, and Willacy located in the southernmost part of
the United States. The authors present the history and
economic development of the region which includes descriptions of early settlements, border conflicts, and the
role of such individuals as Juan Cortina. Covers agriculture, transportation, communications, and industry as
some of the factors which helped developed what at one
time was considered "no man's land" into a thriving,
modern, industrial, and recreational area. Education,

religion, and cultural influences are discussed in a
separate informative chapter.

CG-29 Taylor, Paul Schuster. AN AMERICAN-MEXICAN FRONTIER: NUECES
COUNTY, TEXAS. Chapel Hill: University of North Carolina Press,
1934. 350 p. B & w photos. Field notes. Index. Maps. Tables.

The last part of a study which the writer produced earlier (see CG-30). With a focus on Nueces County he
presents the shifting social and economic fortunes of the
four peoples, Indians, Negroes, Mexicans, and Whites,
who have come in contact and conflict from the time
the Spaniards arrived in 1529 to 1929 when the field
research was completed. Although dated in some respects, it contains revealing chapters of particular interest to Chicanos on labor, agriculture, property ownership, education, and politics.

CG-30 _____. MEXICAN LABOR IN THE UNITED STATES. 3 vols. University of California Publications in Economics, vol. 6, nos. 1-5; vol. 7,
nos. 1-2; vol. 12, nos. 1-3. Berkeley: University of California Press,
1927-29. Field notes. Index. Maps (part fold). Tables.

The first volume consists of a series of five well-documented monographs on different, but related topics.
The term "Mexican" is used irrespective of birthplace.
Details on the monographs follow in the order which
they appear: (1) analyzes the laboring population of
the Imperial Valley--based on field observation done
in 1927; (2) studies the migration to the beet fields in
the valley of the South Platte River in northeastern
Colorado; (3) analyzes migration statistics, pointing out
their misuses and of what value they are; (4) records
the racial statistic for California schools in 1927, showing the numbers and distribution within the state of
children in three ethnic groups (Blacks, Mexican Americans, and Japanese) enrolled in public and Catholic
elementary schools; (5) reveals the findings of the 1929
study concerning the Mexican American labor in Dimmit
County, considered the winter garden district of South
Texas.

Volume II consists of two monographs. The first is a
brief study of a small settlement established at Bethlehem,
Pennsylvania, mostly by Mexican nationals who were con-
tracted to work for the Bethlehem Steel Company. The
findings indicate that these new arrivals were well re-
munerated for their work and accepted by other nation-
alities. Treatment of the Mexican here was far better
than had been the case in the Southwest. The second
monograph is a comprehensive study of the role played
by "Mexicans" in the industrial area comprising Chicago

and the Calumet region. Among the topics covered are labor relations, race relations in industry, Mexican societies, law enforcement domicile, social contacts, and isolation.

The supplementary volume on statistics (vol. 12, 1-3) contains three monographs published in the years 1933-34. The information relating to Mexican Americans in each number is as follows: (1) shows the migration of "Mexicans" into California, indicating their origin by state; (2) contains statistics on the migration to the San Joaquin Valley and the seasonal fluctuation; and (3) statistics on the repatriation of Mexicans in the years 1930-33, the distribution of persons born in Mexico or of Mexican parentage in the United States as shown in the 1930 census, and the region and states from whence they came.

CG-31 Taylor, Ronald B. SWEATSHOPS IN THE SUN: CHILD LABOR ON THE FARM. Foreword by Carey McWilliams. Boston: Beacon Press, 1973. 233 p. Biblio. B & w photos. Index. Notes.

The wretched life of the migrant child and the persistence of this life in the face of an apathetic society is the principle concern of the author. The narrative incorporates the views of both farm workers and growers, but Taylor's sympathy is with the child. Although the problems and conditions described are not restricted to any particular ethnic group, the burden falls most heavily on Chicanos as they make up the largest percentage of any field work force.

CG-32 Wald, Richard A. THE EFFECT OF CULTURAL INFLUENCES ON MEXICAN-AMERICAN CONSUMERS: A COMPARATIVE STUDY OF BUYER BEHAVIOR. San Jose School of Business, Calif.: San Jose State College, 1970. 34 p. App. Biblio. Graphs. Tables. Pap.

Based on questionnaire returns from Santa Clara County, this study provides information relative to Mexican Americans and the influence of their cultural patterns on economic behavior. While not an in-depth study, it does suggest how the Chicano market differs from that of other ethnic groups.

Political Science

CH-1 Castro, Tony. CHICANO POWER: THE EMERGENCE OF MEXICAN AMERICA. New York: Saturday Review Press/E.P. Dutton & Co., 1974. 242 p. Biblio. Index.

A prize-winning journalist presents an objective overview

of the complicated maze of Chicano politics with emphasis on Texas where he is intimately acquainted with the subject. His analysis of La Raza Unida and the impact that this party has had on national and, in particular, southwest politics is an outstanding feature of this book. Another important feature is the author's portrayal of Cesar Chavez, Reies Lopez Tijerina, Rodolfo (Corky) Gonzales, and Jose Angel Gutierrez. The subject is rounded out with information on Chicano history, the beginnings of La Causa and the emergence of the Chicano in the 1960s, and the influence of Black activists and the civil rights movement on the Movimiento.

CH-2 de la Garza, Rudolph O., et al., comps. CHICANOS AND NATIVE AMERICANS: THE TERRITORIAL MINORITIES. Englewood Cliffs, N.J.: Prentice-Hall, 1973. xii, 203 p. Fnn. Tables.

The uniqueness of this reader lies in its emphasis. The editors have brought together unpublished papers on current topics which support their belief that Chicanos and American Indians share common experiences and a relationship with Anglo-American society as no other racial or ethnic groups do. The work is divided into two parts: (1) political inputs (values, attitudes, and political behavior), and (2) political outputs and feedback (how policies are made relative to territorial minorities and the impact of these policies on the target groups).

CH-3 Delgado, Abelardo B. THE CHICANO MOVEMENT: SOME NOT TOO OBJECTIVE OBSERVATIONS. Denver, Colo.: Totinem Publications, 1971. 40 p. B & w photos and draws. Pap.

With emphasis on interpretation and opinion as well as information, the author, in spirited style, gives his personal account of the Movimiento in a series of short essays. Definition, background, scope, goals, strengths, limitations, strategy, and how the movement relates to education, politics, economics, rural areas, and other social spheres are the topics. The viewpoints expressed reflect primarily the author's experiences and observations in Denver, El Paso, and Los Angeles.

CH-4 Endore, Guy. THE SLEEPY LAGOON MYSTERY. n.d. Reprint. San Francisco: R and E Research Associates, 1972. 48 p. B & w photos and draws.

This account, originally published by the Sleepy Lagoon Defense Committee, deals with a true story, probably more difficult to believe than the author's best fiction. On August 2, 1942, the body of Jose Diaz was found dead next to the Sleepy Lagoon, a favorite swimming hole for the poor Chicanos who lived near Slauson and

Atlantic Boulevards in Los Angeles. Members and non-members of the Thirty-eighth Street Gang were arrested and charged with murder. Seventeen out of twenty-two boys were convicted and sent to jail "for a murder that was never even established as a murder." How could this happen? Madness prompted by racial prejudice or more specifically discrimination against Mexican Americans in Southern California was responsible. The verdict was reversed in 1944, but it took a special defense committee headed by Carey McWilliams. It also marked the first organized victory won by Chicanos.

CH-5 Garcia, F. Chris. POLITICAL SOCIALIZATION OF CHICANO CHILDREN: A COMPARATIVE STUDY WITH ANGLOS IN CALIFORNIA SCHOOLS. New York: Praeger Publishers, 1973. 276 p. App. Biblio. Graphs. Tables.

According to Dr. Garcia, a professor of political science at the University of New Mexico, the purpose of this study was to "explore the political orientations of Chicano and Anglo children in order to determine if there are any significant differences in attitudinal attachments in the [American] political system." The findings are based on data collected through a specially-designed questionnaire distributed by trained interviewers in eight California public schools located in the Central Valley of California and East Los Angeles County. Results indicate that Chicanos have a disaffection for America which increases with maturity. The author finds this attitude even more pronounced among Blacks.

CH-6 _____, ed. CHICANO POLITICS: READINGS. New York: MSS Information Corporation, 1973. 225 p.

The readings have been subdivided into four parts. The foundations for Chicano politics are discussed in the first three, primarily from the historical, sociological, and psychological viewpoints. Various selections illustrate the major styles and strategies of politics. The less conventional are included in part IV, which contains EL PLAN DE AZTLAN, and readings on Tijerina, the Brown Berets, and an interview with Cesar Chavez. With few exceptions, the selections are scholarly and written by Chicano subject specialists.

CH-7 Gutierrez, Jose Angel. EL POLITICO: THE MEXICAN AMERICAN ELECTED OFFICIAL. Prospectiva, numero 2. El Paso, Tex.: Mictla Publications, 1972. 63 p. Tables. Pap.

The revolutionary political mentor of the Raza Unida Party has put together a profile of the Mexican American politico on the basis of 165 responses received to

a questionnaire which was directed to Spanish-surnamed
public officials in Texas. Data was obtained on matters
such as campaign methods and techniques used, campaign
costs and distribution. Housewives were identified as
the hardest and most effective campaign workers. Facts
also show that Chicanos have a small voice in the state's
politics and the politico is very similar to other politicians whether Black or white. The appendix consists
of a directory of Spanish-surnamed public officials in
Texas.

CH-8 _____. LA RAZA AND REVOLUTION: THE EMPIRICAL CONDITIONS
OF REVOLUTION IN FOUR SOUTH TEXAS COUNTIES. Thesis, St.
Mary's University, 1968. Reprint. San Francisco: R and E Research
Associates, 1972. vi, 79 p. Biblio. Maps. Tables. Pap.

Could South Texas be struck by revolution? According
to the author, who happens to be the present head of
the Raza Unida political party, the answer is yes. He
comes to this conclusion after finding that the socioeconomic and political conditions of Mexican Americans in
that part of Texas conform to the empirical circumstances
which lead to revolution.

CH-9 Heins, Marjorie. STRICTLY GHETTO PROPERTY: THE STORY OF LOS
SIETE DE LA RAZA. Berkeley, Calif.: Ramparts Press, 1972. 324 p.
B & w draws. & photos. Pap.

This is the inside story about seven Latinos from the
Mission district in San Francisco who nearly were rail-
roaded into prison for the murder of a policeman that
took place on May 1, 1969. The victory of these
young men of Central American origin in the courts
could hardly have come about without the support which
they received from La Raza in the barrio. In narrating
the details of the incident, the author provides background and related information which shows how brown
people can easily become victims of racist institutions
that are responsible for the administration of justice.

CH-10 Lopez y Rivas, Gilberto. LOS CHICANOS: UNA MINORIA NACIO-
NAL EXPLOTADA. Mexico City: Editorial Nuestro Tiempo, 1971.
146 p. Apps. Biblio. Maps. Tables. B & w photos.

This is one of the few scholarly books written by a
Mexican national on the socioeconomic conditions of
Chicanos, to whom it is dedicated. The author observed that the "Mexicano" has been exploited because
he forms a part of a conquered and subjugated minority.
He believes that the roots of the problem are in the
economic base of the United States and its capitalistic
structure. On the one hand the system prevents the

integral development of Chicano people, and on the other it provides for the existence of economic exploitation and discrimination. The three appendices are translations of "Toward an Operational Definition of the Mexican American," by Fernando Penalosa; Dr. Clark S. Knowlton's "Tijerina, Hero of the Militants"; and the epic poem, "I am Joaquin," by Rodolfo Gonzalez.

CH-11 _____. THE CHICANOS: LIFE AND STRUGGLES OF THE MEXICAN MINORITY IN THE UNITED STATES. Translated and edited by Elizabeth Martinez and Gilberto Lopez y Rivas. New York: Monthly Review Press, 1973. 187 p. Apps. Biblio. Tables.

This is a translated version of item CH-10 which remains basically the same as the original. The author has added a brief introduction that is directed to his fellow anthropologists.

CH-12 Macias, Reynaldo F., et al. A STUDY OF UNINCORPORATED EAST LOS ANGELES. Aztlan Publications Monograph, no. 3. Los Angeles: Chicano Studies Center, University of California, 1973. x, 130 p. Apps. Biblio. Maps. Tables.

Why incorporation of the East Los Angeles area? The authors offer the following information: (1) previous attempts at incorporation, (2) the Local Agency Formation Commission (LAFCO), the governmental decision-making body in regard to incorporation, (3) procedures and legal steps to be followed, and (4) socio-statistical data for ELA. The appendices include a bibliography, newspaper excerpts on the reasons for incorporation, a map of the ELA study area, and a list of the public facilities in ELA.

CH-13 Morales, Armando. ANDO SANGRANDO (I AM BLEEDING): A STUDY OF MEXICAN AMERICAN-POLICE CONFLICT. Fair Lawn, N.J.: R. E. Burdick, 1972. ix, 141 p. App. B & w photos. Refs. Tables. Sold by Perspectiva Publications, P.O. Box 3563, La Puente, Calif.

Since responsible authorities would not investigate the causes of the 1970-71 East Los Angeles riots, the Congress of Mexican American Unity and the Chicano Moratorium Committee asked the author to conduct an inquiry into the matter. This documented study indicates that the police force does not perform its duties in the best interests of Chicanos. One chapter discusses in detail the August 19, 1970, riot.

CH-14 Newman, Patty. DO IT UP BROWN! San Diego, Calif.: Viewpoint Books, 1971. 404 p. Index. Pap.

This is a provocative book calculated to arouse an awareness for Chicanismo and the political, socioeconomic movement it represents. Using materials which have appeared in Chicano newspapers and periodicals, the author first identifies the Chicano. This is followed by biographies on Reies Lopez Tijerina, "Corky" Gonzales, and Cesar Chavez. Information is also provided on Chicano organizations such as the Brown Berets, the Young Lords, Venceremos Brigade, MECHA, UMAS, MAYO, LULAC, the G.I. Forum, MAPA, and PASO. Another section gives detailed information on the National Chicano Moratorium Committee and the August 29, 1970, riots in East Los Angeles when Ruben Salazar was killed. The reader is left with the thought that Chicanos are on the move.

CH-15 Rendon, Armando B. CHICANO MANIFESTO. New York: Macmillan Co., 1971. viii, 337 p. App.

The author, who unequivocally identifies himself as a Chicano, has written some rather forceful and well-formulated opinions regarding the history and political and socioeconomic status of Americans of Mexican extraction. In so doing he has captured much of the thought behind Chicanismo. It is a call to action for Chicanos to retain their heritage "by whatever means necessary."

CH-16 Reyes, Ignacio. A SURVEY OF THE PROBLEMS INVOLVED IN THE AMERICANIZATION OF THE MEXICAN AMERICAN. Thesis, University of Southern California, 1957. Reprint. San Francisco: R ane E Research Associates, 1972. v, 61 p. Biblio. Pap.

Through a survey of sample literature on Americanization, the author studies the failure of the majority group in our society to make the Mexican American feel at home in America. The literature surveyed includes books, pamphlets, periodicals, and unpublished materials such as newsletters and master's theses.

CH-17 Santillan, Richard. CHICANO POLITICS: LA RAZA UNIDA. Los Angeles: Tlaquilo Publications, 1973. xii, 179 p. Index. Pap.

Through an in-depth, historical, documented analysis of the new Raza Unida political party, the author traces the long years of struggle by Chicanos to secure a toe-hold in the realm of politics. The existing political parties have taken Chicanos for granted and given them little or nothing in return for their votes. But by 1970 Chicanos were ready to say basta and LRUP was created. The political activism generated by this new party suggests that Chicanos will be playing a more prominent role in the political life of the United States, especially in the Southwest.

CH-18 Shockley, John Staples. CHICANO REVOLT IN A TEXAS TOWN.
Notre Dame: University of Notre Dame Press, 1974. xii, 302 p. Apps.
Biblio. B & w photos. Index. Maps. Tables.

A case study dealing primarily with the ousting of Anglos from political control in Crystal City, first in 1963
when five Chicanos displaced the incumbents on the city
council, and then in 1969 when control of city government and the school system fell to Chicanos under the
banner of the Raza Unida Party, an independent Chicano
political party. Through interviews and information obtained from the local newspaper over the last fifteen
years, the author has written a readable account that
provides historical background and an analysis of the
effect of the change. The subject has been generally
handled with impartiality, but the story has yet to be
told by the Chicanos who were involved. Two appendices worth mentioning are the one containing the peti-
tions presented by high school students to the school
board and the one dealing with the program for bilingual
and bicultural education.

CH-19 U.S. Cabinet Committee on Opportunity for the Spanish Speaking. AN-
NUAL REPORT, FISCAL YEAR 1971. Washington, D.C.: Government
Printing Office, 1971. 120 p. Chart. Map. Tables.

Mostly a progress report with stress on the organizational
structure of the Committee and its responsibilities. The
publication was included in this bibliography primarily
to acquaint those persons who are working with Chicanos
and other Spanish-speaking with the specific efforts made
by the federal agencies represented by the Committee to
resolve matters concerned with the Spanish-speaking
Americans. The reading of this report will point out
the strengths and weaknesses of this government agency
and, in turn, may cause it to be better utilized.

CH-20 U.S. Commission on Civil Rights. MEXICAN AMERICANS AND THE
ADMINISTRATION OF JUSTICE IN THE SOUTHWEST. Washington,
D.C.: Government Printing Office, 1970. 148 p. Apps. Tables.
B & w photos.

This report documents what has been common knowledge
among Mexican Americans. It presents evidence to support findings such as these: (1) police misconduct in the
form of discriminatory and brutal treatment, (2) inadequate protection, (3) interference with Mexican American organizational efforts, (4) inadequacy of local re-
medies for police malpractice, (5) failure of the FBI to
take positive steps to correct the problem, (6) marked
underrepresentation of Mexican Americans on juries, (7)
excessive bail is imposed to punish Mexican Americans

rather than to assure their appearance for trial, and (8) lack of counsel. In addition, this study shows that because some Mexican Americans have a language problem they often become the victims of law enforcement officers and agencies.

CH-21 Woods, Sister Frances Jerome. MEXICAN ETHNIC LEADERSHIP IN SAN ANTONIO, TEXAS. Catholic University of America, Studies in Sociology, vol. 31. Dissertation, Catholic University of America. Washington, D.C.: Catholic University of America Press, 1949. ix, 134 p. Bibliographical Essay. Index. Pap.

Research based mainly on interviews of eighty persons, three-fourths of whom were "Mexican," a term applied to individuals of Mexican ancestry regardless of place of birth or citizenship. Findings reveal that "Mexican" leadership of the patriarchal type changed over the years. The new Raza leadership takes pride in cultural values, but is willing to adopt the Anglo's "attitudes toward work, education, and material comforts." The esteem of his own people as well as the opinions of Anglos is important to the politico. "Mexican" leaders who enjoy the most prestige are sincere and unselfish in their efforts to help La Raza. Some, however, are primarily motivated by monetary and selfish interests. The majority of the Chicano leaders are coming from the middle class. Interesting contrasts with other minority groups are analyzed.

Emigration & Immigration

CH-22 Galarza, Ernesto. MERCHANTS OF LABOR: THE MEXICAN BRACERO STORY. AN ACCOUNT OF THE MANAGED MIGRATION OF MEXICAN FARM WORKERS IN CALIFORNIA, 1942-1960. Preface by Ernest Gruening. Santa Barbara, Calif.: McNally and Loftin Publishers, 1964. 284 p. B & w photos. Biblio.

The epic about Mexicans who continually cross the border--legally and illegally--to work for low wages, mainly in the fields of western United States.

CH-23 Gamio, Manuel. THE MEXICAN IMMIGRANT. 1931. Reprint. New York: Arno Press and the New York Times, 1969. 301 p. Index. Map.

Could be considered a sequel to the author's 1930 MEXICAN IMMIGRATION TO THE UNITED STATES (see CH-24) as the interviewees and the information they provided were the sources of data for the earlier work. The interviews are not considered a scientific study,

but more a source of information which when pieced together sketches a profile not of a particular Mexican
immigrant, but rather "a sort of generalized Mexican
immigrant." Most of the interviewees are male, poor,
unskilled, uneducated, and come from all walks of life
and various parts of Mexico. The material has been
grouped under headings such as economic adjustment,
racial conflict, leadership, and assimilation.

CH-24 _____. MEXICAN IMMIGRATION TO THE UNITED STATES: A STUDY
OF HUMAN MIGRATION AND ADJUSTMENT. Chicago: University of
Chicago Press, 1930. 280 p. Apps. Biblio. Index. Tables.

This study, prepared during 1926-27, has gained importance because it is one of the most comprehensive and
in-depth investigations on the subject and also because
it is prepared by a Mexican anthropologist with an understanding of the problems and people involved. He
shows how the Mexican immigrants were affected by
their contact with the United States and their impact
on the two countries. Includes information on the physical, mental, social, cultural, and economic conditions
of immigrants. The regions from whence they came as
well as the regions in which they lived and worked
while in this country were also studied. Emphasis is
on Mexican nationals, though information on Mexican
Americans is also provided. The work is based on documentary material, personal observation and interviews,
some of which are included. One chapter is devoted
to corridos, the songs of the Mexican immigrant. See
also CH-23.

CH-25 Grebler, Leo, et al. MEXICAN IMMIGRATION TO THE UNITED
STATES: THE RECORD AND ITS IMPLICATIONS. Mexican American
Study Project Advance Report, no. 3. Los Angeles: Division of Research, Graduate School of Business Administration, University of California, 1966. xi, 151 p. Apps. Chap. notes. Graphs. Tables. Pap.

The scope of this study is delimited to selected aspects
of Mexican immigration in the twentieth century. It
provides historical perspectives and discusses distinctive
features which set Mexican immigration apart from earlier
mass movements from Europe. The analysis deals with
demographic and social characteristics of the immigrants
and their geographic distribution in the United States.
Information is further provided on temporary and permanent migrations. The study closes with views on the
future which suggest that since economic conditions in
Mexico cannot improve fast enough, the propensity to
move north will continue among disadvantaged Mexicans.

CH-26 Hoffman, Abraham. UNWANTED MEXICAN AMERICANS IN THE GREAT DEPRESSION. REPATRIATION PRESSURES, 1929-1939. Tucson: University of Arizona Press, 1974. 222 p. Apps. Biblio. B & w photos. Maps. Source notes. Tables.

Originally the subject of a dissertation, this work partially fills in a period of time that has been neglected by American historians, probably because the repatriation of over 400,000 Mexicans and their American-born children is equated with the shameful treatment of American Indians and the relocation of Japanese in the 1940s. The author deals primarily with what happened in Los Angeles County--the hardest hit area. Indications suggest, however, that the expulsion of Mexicans, and to a lesser degree other aliens, also took place across the nation, particularly at the height of the depression. The story behind the repatriation amounts to a self-serving device employed by the white, Anglo-Saxon, middle class against people whom they used to their advantage, but rejected in a time of economic crisis.

CH-27 Martinez, John. MEXICAN EMIGRATION TO THE U.S. 1910-1930. Dissertation, University of California at Berkeley, 1957. Reprint. San Francisco: R and E Research Associates, 1971. v. 100 p. Biblio.

This study shows that prior to 1910 relatively few Mexicans immigrated to this country. The large emigrations after that date were propelled by the Revolution itself. The subsequent poor economy of Mexico coincided with the American agricultural expansion which provided almost unlimited work opportunities. The emigration after 1930 is not included in this work because the author finds it different in various aspects and merits a separate study.

CH-28 Samora, Julian. LOS MOJADOS: THE WETBACK STORY. Assisted by Jorge A. Bustamante F. and Gilbert Cardenas. Notre Dame: University of Notre Dame Press, 1971. 205 p. Biblio. B & w photos. Graphs. Index. Maps. Tables.

With sympathy for his subject, yet observing the rules for scientific research, the author, a sociologist, gives a grim and detailed account of a group of people who are continually entering the United States illegally, often taking dangerous risks and suffering abuse in their search for the American dollar.

CH-29 Santibanez, Enrique. ENSAYO ACERCA DE LA INMIGRACION MEXICANA EN LOS ESTADOS UNIDOS. San Antonio, Tex.: The Clegg Co., 1930. 105 p. Index. Tables.

The content of this book originally appeared as a series

of articles in the Mexican newspaper, EXCELSIOR, when
the author was the Counsel General of Mexico in San
Antonio. The significance of the work is that it represents one of the few accounts of that time written by
a Mexican about Mexicans and Mexican Americans. Of
special interest are his remarks about Texas history, but
the emphasis is on the different Mexican migrations.
He discusses such topics as the living and working conditions of farmworkers, racial prejudices, and the pros
and cons of Mexican immigration. In a brief chapter
he paints a rather dismal picture of Mexican Americans.

HISTORY

HISTORY

Bibliography

DA-1 Journal of Mexican American History. MEXICAN AMERICAN HISTORY: A CRITICAL SELECTIVE BIBLIOGRAPHY. Santa Barbara, Calif.: Mexican American Historical Society, 1969. 30 p. Pap.

> Arranged into three major divisions, the first being a brief introduction by Carey McWilliams and two separate sections which contain titles arranged alphabetically by author under broad subject headings and subheadings. Part II provides background materials which include general monographs about the indigenous American peoples and culture, the history of Spain and Mexico, as well as the Spanish borderlands and United States imperialism. Part III is devoted to writings about Mexican American history, 1848 to 1969, and includes books, periodical articles, theses, and official publications. Only a very few titles are followed by a one-sentence evaluative statement or a descriptive term such as "basic" or "excellent." All other entries are neither annotated nor do they include a collation. Publications available in paperback are indicated by an asterisk. The work can be considered adequate for beginners in Chicano history, but specialists will need to consult bibliographic sources with more depth and breadth.

DA-2 Meier, Matt S., and Rivera, Feliciano. A BIBLIOGRAPHY FOR CHICANO HISTORY. San Francisco: R & E Research Associates, 1972. iii, 96 p. Pap.

> This chronologically arranged, unannotated bibliography lists selected "items useful to understand each of the major historical periods from the Mexican American's origin to the present day struggles for justice." There are three topical divisions: labor and immigration, Chicano culture, and civil rights. Includes books, government documents, pamphlets, periodical articles, masters'

theses and doctoral dissertations. The latter are listed
separately. The last section is a bibliography of Mexican American bibliographies. Designed for use by teachers, students, and librarians.

DA-3   Rivera, Feliciano.   A MEXICAN AMERICAN SOURCE BOOK.   Menlo
Park, Calif.:   Educational Consulting Associates, 1970.   xi, 196 p.
App.   Biblio.   Draws.   Lithographs.   Ports.   Reprods. of orig. paintings
in b & w.

Intended as a guideline to the history of the Chicano,
in actuality it is a multi-purpose book which combines
several types of information. Its assortment is so varied
that it gives the impression of a haphazard catch-all.
It begins with a history of the Chicano in outline form.
Then follows a short, partially annotated bibliography,
a list of Chicano newspapers, films, and filmstrips. The
next major section includes an excerpt from MISSIONS
OF CALIFORNIA (published in 1970 by P G & E Company of San Francisco). Next is an impressive pictorial
section intended to illustrate 400 years of Spanish culture in the Southwest. An English-Spanish WHO'S WHO
of outstanding Mexican Americans is included also. Of
the more important items contained in the last portion is
a reprint of the Treaty of Guadalupe Hidalgo. Considering its limitations, this book can be a useful reference tool, particularly to beginners in Chicano studies.
See item AA-5 for the basis of this work.

Biography

DA-4   Blawis, Patricia Bell.   TIJERINA AND THE LAND GRANTS: MEXICAN
AMERICANS IN STRUGGLE FOR THEIR HERITAGE.   New York: International Publishers, 1971.   191 p.   App.   B & w photos.   Index.   Ref.
notes.

As the story of Reies Lopez Tijerina is narrated, the
author describes the events leading to his emergence
as a leader. The New Mexican land grant issue is
placed in historical context, tracing its origin and the
plight of Mexican Americans to the war against Mexico.
The book ends with Tijerina still in jail, but points to
evidence that indicates the fight is not yet over.

DA-5   Burns, Walter Noble.   THE ROBIN HOOD OF EL DORADO: THE SAGA
OF JOAQUIN MURRIETA, FAMOUS OUTLAW OF CALIFORNIA'S AGE
OF GOLD.   New York: Coward-McCann, 1932.   304 p.

The author of BILLY THE KID presents his version of
the legendary outlaw who gained notoriety during the

years of the Gold Rush. To give veracity to the narrative, the writer footnotes a few specific passages.
Also, he refers to the work of John Ridge who originally
wrote the Murrieta story. This account is basically the
same as that written by Ridge, but is more readable and
provides more details on the setting and the people involved.

DA-6 Castillo, Pedro, and Camarillo, Albert, eds. FURIA Y MUERTE: LOS
BANDIDOS CHICANOS. Introduction by editors. Chicano Studies
Center Monograph, no. 4. Los Angeles: Aztlan Publications, Univer-
sity of California, 1973. vii, 171 p. Ports. Sugg. reads.

The text includes reprinted scholarly selections which
depict the life and activities of the following legendary
Chicano heroes: Tiburcio Vasquez, Joaquin Murrieta,
Elfego Baca, Juan N. Cortina, and Gregorio Cortez.
With the exception of the piece on Cortez, all others
are written by Anglo authors. In the introduction the
editors, as historians, examine for the first time the
social banditry which came about in defiance of the
Anglo's invasion of the Southwest.

DA-7 Dawson, Joseph Martin. JOSE ANTONIO NAVARRO: CO-CREATOR
OF TEXAS. Waco, Tex.: Baylor University Press, 1969. 141 p. B
& w photos. Index. Gloss.

In writing this well-documented biography of an Angli-
cized Mexican hero who has been neglected by historians, the author has drawn a detailed portrait of a man
who, like Sam Houston and Stephen F. Austin, was at
the forefront of Texas independence. Contains historical data relative to the Texas-Mexico conflict and San
Antonio where Navarro was born in 1795.

DA-8 Gardner, Richard. GRITO! REIES TIJERINA AND THE NEW MEXICO
LAND GRANT WAR OF 1967. New York: Harper & Row, Harper
Colophon Books, 1970. 292 p. Biblio. B & w photos. Pap.

Grito, a term which recalls the resounding cry of 1810
for Mexican independence, in this case is used sym-
bolically in reference to the courthouse raid in Tierra
Amarilla. The author skillfully weaves a detailed and
factual story of the man who organized the Alianza
Federal de Mercedes and led the land grant war in New
Mexico, with historical and current information regarding
state politics and the conditions of the Hispanos that
prompted this significant event.

DA-9 Gomez-Quinones, Juan. SEMBRADORES: RICARDO FLORES MAGON
Y EL PARTIDO LIBERAL MEXICANO: A EULOGY AND CRITIQUE.

Chicano Studies Center Monograph, no. 5. Los Angeles: Aztlan Publications, University of California, 1973. vii, 172 p. Biblio. B & w
photos. Ports.

In writing about the author of SEMBRANDO IDEAS
(probably the source that inspired the title of this work),
Prof. Gomez-Quinones has put together a documented
biography which narrates highlights in the life of Ricardo
Flores Magon and his Partido Liberal Mexicano which
he founded in the United States in 1904. Further light
is cast on this revolutionary thinker and anarchist through
REGENE-RACION, the radical newspaper which he also
helped to establish. Though Flores Magon came to this
country to escape the Porfiriato and his writings and
political efforts were particularly directed to effect a
social change in Mexico, the author emphasizes his
activities in the Southwest and his influence on Chicanos of his day. The appendix includes editorials, articles, manifestos, and letters written by Flores Magon.

DA-10 Jenkinson, Michael. TIJERINA: LAND GRANT CONFLICT IN NEW
MEXICO. Albuquerque, N. Mex.: Paisano Press, 1968. 104 p. B &
w photos. Map. Port. Pap.

Interviews with Tijerina made it possible for this English-
born author who has lived much of his life in California
and New Mexico to draw a particular portrait of the
man who kindled new expectations among the Hispano
villagers who over the years had lost their land to the
Anglos. Though this is not a documented study, it
includes informative historical background on the ancient land-grant struggle and chronicles the events which
finally culminated in the Tierra Amarilla courthouse raid
of 1967, causing mobilization of the National Guard,
state police, and mounted patrol. The narrative is
graphic but dispassionate, yet shows that injustices need
to be amended.

DA-11 Nabokov, Peter. TIJERINA AND THE COURTHOUSE RAID. Albuquerque: University of New Mexico Press, 1969. xii, 285 p. Biblio. B
& w photos. Maps. Index.

This is an account of the now famous courthouse raid in
Tierra Amarilla, the events that brought it about, and
its immediate ramifications. The author also narrates
Tijerina's personal history and facts about the movement
which he led. Tijerina's trial is covered in the epi-
logue. The bulk of the documentation is drawn from
newspapers.

DA-12 Otero, Miguel Antonio. MY LIFE ON THE FRONTIER, 1864-1882: IN-

CIDENTS AND CHARACTERS OF THE PERIOD WHEN KANSAS, COLO-
RADO, AND NEW MEXICO WERE PASSING THROUGH THE LAST OF
THEIR WILD AND ROMANTIC YEARS. Vol. 1. New York: Press of
the Pioneers, 1935. 293 p. Index.

Annotation follows next entry.

DA-13 _____. MY LIFE ON THE FRONITER, 1882-1897: DEATH KNELL OF
A TERRITORY AND BIRTH OF A STATE. Vol. 2. Foreword by George
P. Hammond. Albuquerque: University of New Mexico Press, 1939.
xi, 306 p. B & w ports. Index.

This two-volume narrative will be a disappointment to
those persons looking for readings that engender pride
in their Hispanic/Mexican heritage. The account is an
Anglo production in style, content, and point of view.
A partial explanation may be found in the author's ancestry. On his father's side his grandparents were Hispanos, but his mother's lineage is traced to one of the
signers of the Declaration of Independence. Coming
from a prominent New Mexican family, he socialized
with the elite, and particularly with the Anglo-American high society. The gente de razon who were con-
scious of their social status found it convenient to side
with the Anglos after 1848 and to adopt their ways.
Otero's recollections are divided into two parts. In
the first volume he dramatizes the frontier in the manner of a Hollywood saga. He thrives on graphic details which depict exciting moments and bad characters.
Every gunslinger of the time, including Buffalo Bill,
Kit Carson, and Jesse James, is mentioned as his ac-
quaintance. The second volume relates important events
in the author's life including his political career and
particularly the nine years he served as the governor of
the Territory of New Mexico. A few pages are devoted
to the Penitentes and the Gorras Blancas for all of whom
he exhibited little sympathy.

DA-14 Paz, Ireneo. LIFE AND ADVENTURES OF THE CELEBRATED BANDIT,
JOAQUIN MURRIETA: HIS EXPLOITS IN THE STATE OF CALIFORNIA.
Translated by Frances P. Belle. Chicago: Regan Publishing Corp.,
1925. x, 174 p.

This story is similar to the one first written by Ridge
(see John Rollin Ridge). Murrieta was beaten by greedy,
wicked Anglos because he refused to give up his rich
mining claim. As for his wife, "...after subjecting
her to the worst indignities imaginable they took her
life." Sometime after this incident he was accused of
horse stealing. Unsuccessful in convincing his accusers
of his innocence, he was shamefully beaten in public.
From that time on he lived only for revenge. Most of

the book is concerned with the plunder that followed. The author states that his account is based on "authentic facts and documents almost official." But then he adds, "Sometimes, perhaps, we have given some color to the deeds."

DA-15 Ridge, John Rollin [Yellow Bird]. THE LIFE AND ADVENTURES OF JOAQUIN MURRIETA. THE CELEBRATED CALIFORNIA BANDIT. 1854. Reprint. Introduction by Joseph Henry Jackson. Norman: University of Oklahoma Press, 1955. 159 p. B & w draws. Ports.

The author, a Cherokee Indian, narrated the story with the idea of contributing to the early history of California. He tells how the Sonoran-born Murrieta robbed and killed during the day of the California Gold Rush to avenge the injuries suffered at the hands of rapacious, Anglo frontiersmen. In the introduction the story is said to be a myth invented by Ridge in vengence for the mistreatment of his people and the violence inflicted upon his own family.

History - General

DA-16 Acuna, Rodolfo. OCCUPIED AMERICA: THE CHICANO'S STRUGGLE TOWARD LIBERATION. San Francisco: Harper & Row, Canfield Press, 1972. vi, 282 p. Chap. notes. Index. Pap.

Based on research, the author presents an authoritative, historical overview of happenings in the Southwest during the last 124 years to support his thesis that Mexican Americans are a colonized people in the United States. The first half of the book concentrates primarily on the conquest and colonization which took place in the nineteenth century. The second half is devoted to the Chicano experience in the twentieth century.

DA-17 Alford, Harold J. THE PROUD PEOPLES: THE HERITAGE AND CULTURE OF SPANISH-SPEAKING PEOPLES IN THE UNITED STATES. New York: David McKay Co., 1972. 325 p. Biblio. Index.

Written in layman's language, this history dramatizes the events and contributions, as well as the problems, needs, and potential of the Spanish-speaking/Spanish-surnamed people in the country. About a fourth of the book is devoted to biographical sketches of Cuban Americans, Mexican Americans, Puerto Ricans, and Spanish who have distinguished themselves in government, business, education, sports, arts, and other fields of endeavor. A few biographies are of individuals of the past. No systematic criteria for selection was used.

DA-18 Brophy, A. Blake. FOUNDLINGS ON THE FRONTIER. RACIAL AND RELIGIOUS CONFLICT IN ARIZONA TERRITORY, 1904-1905. Tucson: University of Arizona Press, 1972. xii, 129 p. B & w photos. Index. Notes. Pap.

> This is a true story that Cliftonites would probably like to forget. Hell broke loose in the Anglo community of Clifton, Arizona, in 1904, when fifty-seven Anglo children arrived in that town from the New York Foundling Hospital to be placed in Mexican American homes. Since the Anglos felt that the "greasers" were not suitable foster parents for the white orphans, most of the children had to be sent back to New York. Seventeen of the children were adopted by Anglos who were awarded custody by a biased court.

DA-19 Bustamante, Charles J., and Bustamante, Patricia L. THE MEXICAN AMERICAN AND THE UNITED STATES. Illustrated by Sam Sanchez. Mountain View, Calif.: Patty-Lar Publications, 1969. 60 p. Biblio. B & w draws. Pap.

> Written as an intermediate level text, this simplified account traces the history of Chicanos from the early peoples who populated the lands which became Spain and pre-Columbian Mexico to the Delano farm workers' strike. Because of the readability and elemental presentation of the subject, this book will have appeal to persons who desire easy reading in this particular field.

DA-20 Castaneda, Carlos Eduardo. OUR CATHOLIC HERITAGE IN TEXAS, 1519-1936. Supplement 1936-1950. 7 vols. Prepared under auspices of the Knights of Columbus of Texas. Austin: Von Boeckmann-Jones Co., Publishers, 1936-58. Apps. Biblio. Index. Ports. Plates. Fold maps.

> Many are the writings of the late Dr. Castaneda who distinguished himself as a scholar and teacher in the field of Latin American history. His principal contribution as a historian is this multi-volumed work which serves as a testimony of scholarship and the author's veritable devotion to his faith. In the first six volumes he has narrated what is considered to be the most complete history of Texas. This account is effectively interwoven with the part played by the church in the state's development and growth. Contrary to what the title might suggest, only the last volume is devoted to the history of the church. To facilitate use of this work, a glimpse of each volume is offered:
>
> Vol. 1 covers the history of Texas from 1519 to 1694. Deals with early explorations such as La Salle's expedition and the beginnings of missionary activity, including

the establishment of missions in east Texas. One chapter
is devoted to the tragic story of the four Dominican
Friars who were shipwrecked on what is now Padre Island.

Vol. 2 covers the period from 1694 to 1714. It deals
with an account of permanent occupation of Texas and
the development of mission life.

Vol. 3 concentrates on the middle eighteenth century,
providing details on the area covered by the present
Presidio to El Paso and the Lower Rio Grande Valley.
Information is also provided on the Texas Indians and
the hostile Apaches.

Vol. 4 covers 1762 to 1782. Deals with topics previously mentioned, but which are treated in depth and/
or expanded with new information. Sample topics are
the withdrawal of Queretaran missionaires from Texas
and the beginning of secularization.

Vol. 5 considers the years 1780 to 1810 when the mission era officially came to an end and the last new
mission was founded in the northern frontier of New
Spain. The narrative also covers the impact suffered
by Texas as a result of the Louisiana Purchase in 1803.

Vol. 6 covers 1810 to 1936. The principal topics are
the revolt of the Spanish colonies, deterioration of the
Catholic Church, and its effect on the missions, the
colonization of Texas by Anglo-Americans, and the conflict which culminated in a revolution and lead to an
independent republic.

Vol. 7, which starts with 1936 and ends in 1950, is
restricted mainly to the history of the Church since
Texas independence. It describes its growth, development, and contributions made to the state and its people. Gives detailed information on the Knights of
Columbus.

DA-21 Connor, Seymour V., and Faulk, Odie B. NORTH AMERICA DIVIDED:
THE MEXICAN WAR, 1846-1848. New York: Oxford University Press,
1971. 313 p. Biblio. Index.

The authors feel that previous histories were written,
whether by Mexicans or Americans, with preconceived
inclinations. This work is their attempt to place the
event in its nineteenth-century setting as well as re-
evaluate the voluminous scholarship of the Mexican War
without twentieth-century biases. The twist is that the
guilt for the war should lie not with either nation, but
rather on the "men and political factions" of the time.
This scholarly account is presented without footnotes,
but is accompanied by an impressive analytical bibliography.

DA-22 Davis, W.W.H. EL GRINGO--OR NEW MEXICO AND HER PEOPLE.
Drawings by Brevet Lt. Col. Eaton, U.S.A. and F.A. Percy, Esq. New
York: Harper & Bros., 1857. xii, 432 p. B & w draws.

Based on his personal observations and a diary he kept
for two and a half years, the author, an attorney, tells
of his journey from Independence, Missouri, to New
Mexico in 1853. Interesting descriptions of the people
and the land in Santa Fe and surrounding area as seen
through the eyes of an Anglo stranger to the region.
His account of the Pueblo Indians and the description
of the Hispanos' life style, with emphasis on their manners and customs, makes fascinating and informative
reading.

DA-23 Faulk, Odie B., and Stout, Joseph A., Jr., eds. THE MEXICAN WAR:
CHANGING INTERPRETATIONS. Chicago: Swallow Press, 1973. 244
p. Index. Maps. Tables.

Different aspects of the Mexican conflict are presented
through articles written by subject specialists which first
appeared in the JOURNAL OF THE WEST. Each selection forms a separate chapter and is introduced by a
summary statement. One of the chapter authors, Seymour V. Connor, did a quantitative analysis of the
causes of the war and opinions held in different socio-
political periods about the War. Categorizing some 766
books, pamphlets, and articles into a computer program,
he produced statistics which seem to indicate that "there
is no basis for the flagellation of Americans of the 1840s
for the war with Mexico."

DA-24 Gonzalez, Nancie L. Solien. THE SPANISH-AMERICANS OF NEW
MEXICO: A HERITAGE OF PRIDE. Rev. and enl. ed. Albuquerque:
University of New Mexico Press, 1969. 261 p. B & w photos. Bib-
lio. Index. Map.

An account of the sociocultural system of the New Mexico Hispanos. The author describes this culture "both as
functioning subsystem and in relation to the broader society of which it is an integral part."

DA-25 Horgan, Paul. CONQUISTADORES IN NORTH AMERICAN HISTORY.
New York: Farrar, Straus and Co., 1963. 318 p. Biblio. Index.

A modern history of the Conquistadores from Columbus to
Cortes, and including such personalities as Nunez de
Cabez de Vaca, Coronado, Onate, Vargas, and the
Marquess of La Nava Brazinas who died in New Mexico
in 1704. By consulting published documents for background information of actual events, the novelist has
written in his characteristic expressive style a readable

narrative which interprets the two-century Spanish conquest as one in which the conquerors were driven by
strong personal desires to gain wealth and glory for
themselves as well as honor for the Spanish Crown by
bringing new lands and peoples under its authority.

DA-26 Kibbe, Pauline R. LATIN AMERICANS IN TEXAS. Albuquerque: University of New Mexico Press, 1946. 323 p. App. Biblio. B & w
photos. Index.

Use of the term "Latin Americans" instead of Chicanos
could suggest that the work is outdated. However, what
changes have taken place in the socioeconomic conditions of Mexican Americans are so limited that much of
what was written twenty-eight years ago can still prove
useful to the discerning reader. Among the problems
dealt with are social and civil inequalities, economic
evils, education, migratory labor, prejudices, housing,
health, and nutrition.

DA-27 Lamb, Ruth Stanton. MEXICAN AMERICANS: SONS OF THE SOUTH-
WEST. Claremont. Calif.: Ocelot Press, 1970. 198 p. Biblio. Maps.

A concise account that traces the historical background
of Mexican Americans up to the present day. The
Treaty of Guadalupe Hidalgo and the Gadsden Treaty
are reprinted with comments. An extensive bibliography
reflects general and specialized subjects including literature in translation, interpretations, and children's literature. Both English and Spanish language materials.

DA-28 Lowrie, Samuel Harman. CULTURE CONFLICT IN TEXAS, 1821-1835.
New York: AMS Press, 1967. 189 p. Biblio. Index.

The author contends that the conflict between Mexicans
and Anglos developed from misunderstandings which came
about over differences in folkways and mores, religion,
and incompatible cultural patterns of the two groups.
He discards geography, racial differences, and the status
of the Mexican nation as primary sources of friction.
The analysis is based on sociological principles.

DA-29 McWilliams, Carey. THE MEXICANS IN AMERICA: A STUDENT'S
GUIDE TO LOCALIZED HISTORY. New York: Teachers College Press,
Columbia University, 1968. vii, 32 p. Biblio. Pap.

Although this is but a bird's-eye view, the author summarizes a great deal of information in his characteristi-
cally forceful style. He discusses history, Mexican immigrations, and various aspects which make Mexican
Americans "a special minority." Further, he explains

their contributions to the nation and the subtle discrimination against this group as well as the long-standing government neglect which has placed Chicanos at a socioeconomic disadvantage. In commenting on the stirrings that have been taking place in the Southwest, McWilliams states that "Spanish-Mexican influence will survive."

DA-30 Meier, Matt S., and Rivera, Feliciano. THE CHICANOS: A HISTORY OF THE MEXICAN AMERICAN. American Century Series. New York: Hill and Wang, 1972. 320 p. Biblio. Index.

A historical approach beginning with the Indo-Hispanic period and concluding with contemporary events. The authors cover the movement of Mexicans into the Southwest and the post World War I acceleration in the use of and exploitation of Mexicans as farm laborers. Also included are accounts of the activities of such people as "Corky" Gonzales, Jose Angel Gutierrez, Reies Lopez Tijerina, and Cesar Chavez. Especially recommended for public and college libraries.

DA-31 _____, eds. READINGS ON LA RAZA -- THE TWENTIETH CENTURY. New York: Hill and Wang, 1974. 295 p. Map.

The editors have selected previously published materials written by both Anglos and Mexican Americans such as articles, reports, speeches, excerpts from books, theses, and dissertations, and arranged the selections chronologically to give the reader various perspectives on "what has happened to Chicanos since 1900." Several controversial events and issues are presented, e.g., the repatriation of the 1930s, the "zoot-suit" riots, "Operation Wetback," and the Movimiento of the sixties spearheaded by Rodolfo Gonzalez, Reies Lopez Tijerina, and Jose Angel Gutierrez. Also there is a brief essay on the Mexican American woman.

DA-32 Moquin, Wayne, and Van Doren, Charles, eds. A DOCUMENTARY HISTORY OF THE MEXICAN AMERICANS. Introduction by Feliciano Rivera, consulting ed. New York: Praeger, 1971. 413 p. B & w photos.

Consists of sixty-five readings which document the history of the Mexican American people from 1536 to 1970. The book is further divided into five chapters, each one representing a significant epoch in the progression of events. Includes the text of the Treaty of Guadalupe.

DA-33 Mora, Jo. CALIFORNIOS: THE SAGA OF THE HARD-RIDING VA-

QUEROS, AMERICA'S FIRST COWBOYS. Illustrated by author. New York: Doubleday & Co., 1949. 175 p. B & w draw.

A vaquero of yesteryear traces the story of the Alta California cowboys from the first Spanish mission corrals to the arrival of the Anglo frontiersmen, when the vaquero was "taken for a ride" and "...relieved of his ranchos, his horses, and his cattle, legally or otherwise, by many of the invading 'wolves'." The prose which describes the early Californian horseman at work and play, together with his customs, mounts and equipment, is greatly enhanced by the graphic drawings.

DA-34 Nava, Julian. MEXICAN AMERICANS: PAST, PRESENT, AND FUTURE. New York: American Book Co., 1969. viii, 120 p. Biblio. B & w photos. Maps. Ports.

Traces the history of Mexican Americans and describes the social, political, and cultural contributions made by this ethnic group in the United States. The language and overall format suggests the work is intended as a textbook for junior high school students.

DA-35 _____. VIVA LA RAZA! READINGS ON MEXICAN AMERICANS. New York: D. Van Nostrand Co., 1973. 183 p. Index. Graphs. Tables.

The author, a historian, has prepared a simplified, comprehensive history which begins by describing the Indo-Hispanic civilizations and continues with a range of topics from the conflict of cultures in the Southwest before and after 1848 up to the present day problems of Chicanos concerning economics, education, politics, and immigration. It appropriately ends with the poem, "I Am Joaquin," which dramatically recapitulates the Chicano experience. The arrangement of the content and readability suggest that it should have special appeal for high school and beginning college students.

DA-36 Pitt, Leonard. THE DECLINE OF THE CALIFORNIOS: A SOCIAL HISTORY OF THE SPANISH-SPEAKING CALIFORNIANS, 1846-1890. Berkeley and Los Angeles: University of California Press, 1966. x, 324 p. Biblio. B & w photos. Gloss. Index.

This scholarly account deals primarily with the Spanish-speaking of Southern California. It begins with the arrival of the Mexican Governor Jose Maria Echeandie and ends with the period when the Californios lost their political hold and the ranchos were subdivided into farms and towns. Main emphasis is on the native-born Californians and their families. Some attention given to Mexican immigrants.

DA-37 Price, Glenn W. ORIGINS OF THE WAR WITH MEXICO: THE POLK-STOCKTON INTRIGUE. Austin: University of Texas Press, 1967. x, 189 p. Biblio. Index.

Attempts to establish the covert stratagem devised between the expansionist President, James Polk, and the unscrupulous Commodore Robert F. Stockton to provoke the war with Mexico. Both primary and secondary sources document this work. The former includes the correspondence of Commodore Stockton.

DA-38 Rojas, Arnold R. THE VAQUERO. Illustrated by Nicholas S. Firfires. Charlotte, N.C.: McNally and Loftin, Publishers, 1964. 207 p.

Fifty years in the saddle provide ample credentials for this writer to describe the life of the vaquero or buckaroo (vaquero--bukeras--buckaroo). This work is based on the author's personal knowledge and experience and information contributed by the few remaining "old timers" who still remembered the tradition and history of the western horseman. Included are short essays on such topics as the difference between the cowboy and the vaquero, the Baja, California, vaquero, the "Spanish California dialect," as well as the vaquero's saddle and bridle. These are followed by folk tales, character sketches, legends, and simple narratives told by or about the buckaroos.

DA-39 Ruiz, Ramon Eduardo, ed. THE MEXICAN WAR: WAS IT MANIFEST DESTINY? New York: Holt, Rinehart and Winston, 1963. 118 p.

A reader which presents diverse points of view on the controversial Mexican War. With the exception of two selections by Mexicans and one by a German historian, all other selections are written by Americans. There are American historians who blame the war on the South, or explain the conflict in terms of Manifest Destiny, or who point the finger at individuals such as Polk. For Justo Sierra, the notable statesman and writer of the postwar generation, the blame lies with unscrupulous politicians and church officials, a blundering military cast, and the self-interested upper class. Interestingly, Ruiz notes in his introduction that while Americans have relegated the war to the past, the Mexicans have not yet forgotten it.

DA-40 Sanchez Lamego, Miguel A. THE SIEGE & TAKING OF THE ALAMO. Translated by Consuelo Velasco. Some comments on the battle by J. Hefter. Santa fe, N. Mex.: Blue Feather Press for Press of the Territorian, 1968. 53 p.

A Mexican general presents the official Mexican version

of the famous military episode with facts derived from
research of documents housed in the Historical Archives
of the National Defense of Mexico. In writing the
Mexican's side of the story, the author provides new
insights and a perspective different from the one commonly accepted in this country. Includes a brief account of the death of David Crockett. Also an unsung
hero is brought to light--Sub-Lieutenant Jose Maria
Torres.

DA-41 Santa Anna, Antonio Lopez de., pres. Mexico, 1794?-1876. THE MEXI-
CAN SIDE OF THE TEXAN REVOLUTION (1836) BY THE CHIEF MEXI-
CAN PARTICIPANTS: D. RAMON MARTINEX CARO, SECRETARY TO
SANTA ANNA; GENERAL VICENTE FILISOLA; GENERAL JOSE URREA;
GENERAL JOSE MARIA TORNEL, SECRETARY OF WAR. Translated with
notes by Carlos E. Castaneda. Illustrated by Carol Rogers and Jim Box.
2nd ed. Austin, Tex.: Graphic Ideas Inc., 1970. xi, 402 p. B &
w draws. Index.

The events and circumstances which climaxed in the
independence of Texas are described in five documents.
Santa Anna writes of his operations in the Texas campaign and his capture. The secretary to Santa Anna
gives an account of the first Texas campaign and the
events that followed the Battle of San Jacinto. General Vicente Filisola renders an account of his military
and political conduct as general-in-chief of the Army
of Texas. General Jose Urrea refutes charges against
him by presenting the diary of his military operations.
Tornel narrates the relations between Texas, the United
States, and Mexico.

DA-42 Servin, Manuel P. THE MEXICAN AMERICANS: AN AWAKENING
MINORITY. Beverly Hills, Calif.: Glencoe Press, 1970. vii, 235 p.
Biblio.

A comprehensive historical overview of Mexican Americans. Includes six new historical studies in addition to
various previously published selections. Contains references that date to the sixteenth century, but emphasis
is on the last fifty years. Treats in chronological order
the racial, cultural, educational, economic, and political development of the Mexican American in the United
States.

DA-43 Singletary, Otis A. THE MEXICAN WAR. Chicago: University of
Chicago Press, 1960. vii, 181 p. B & w photos. Index. Maps.

A biased account in which the author claims the war
with Mexico was motivated by more than "land hunger."
Its broader implications involved Mexico's political in-

stability, the hostility many Americans felt for Mexico,
U.S. politics of the time, and President Polk's own
shortcomings.

DA-44 Stowell, Jay S. THE NEAR SIDE OF THE MEXICAN QUESTION. New
York: George H. Doran Co., 1921. 123 p.

Though the title may not suggest the real topic of the
book, it is mainly the Mexican Americans in the Southwest. The work is dated, but makes interesting reading
as the author writes with understanding about "a group
which has become well-nigh indispensable to our national
life and one with which we must reckon in the days to
come." Religion and education are among the principal subjects discussed. One whole chapter is devoted
to the Spanish-Americans of New Mexico.

DA-45 Sutherland Martinez, Elizabeth, and Longeaux y Vasquez, Enriqueta.
VIVA LA RAZA! THE STRUGGLE OF THE MEXICAN AMERICAN PEO-
PLE. Introduction by Mae Durham Roger. Garden City, N.Y.: Double-
day and Co., 1974. viii, 353 p. Index.

The coauthors, both of whom have been active in the
Movimiento, shed that feminine demure which is so often attributed to the mujer mexicana, and aggressively
tackle the interpretation of Chicano history from their
vantage point. Their forthright narrative acquaints the
reader with the Chicano's Indian heritage as well as
the arrival of the Conquistadores and contemporary events
concerning the Chicano. Included are highlights about
individuals such as Juan Cortina, Joaquin Murrieta,
Tiburcio Vasquez, and Elfego Baca, all who in the
course of history bravely fought against Anglo oppres-
sion. The contributions to La Causa by persons such
as Rodolfo (Corky) Gonzales, Cesar Chavez, Reies Lopez Tijerina, and Jose Angel Gutierrez are also described. A well-researched account that is readable
and convincing.

DA-46 Twitchell, Ralph Emerson. THE CONQUEST OF SANTA FE, 1846.
Edited by Bill Tate. Truchas, N. Mex.: Tate Gallery, 1967. 73 p.
B & w photos.

A historical account narrated from the Anglo's viewpoint
and based on the Magoffin Papers. Provides details about
the occupation of Santa Fe. James Magoffin, who was
born in Kentucky and later became a wealthy business-
man in Chihuahua, was the U.S. secret agent who prepared the way for General Stephen Watts Kearny's
bloodless invasion of New Mexico.

DA-47 Vega, Jose J. NUESTRA AMERICA: CAPITULOS OLVIDADOS DE
NUESTRA HISTORIA...vol. 1, hasta 1848. Mexico City: Impresora
Galve, 1969. 253 p. Biblio. App. Gloss. Illus. Maps.

A historical account of early discoveries, explorations,
heroic feats, and the colonization undertaken by individuals of Mexican or Spanish origin seldom mentioned in
American history books.

DA-48 Vigil, Antonio S. THE COMING OF THE GRINGO (AY VIENEN LOS
GRINGOS!) AND THE MEXICAN AMERICAN REVOLT. AN ANALY-
SIS OF THE RISE AND DECLINE OF ANGLO-AMERICA, U.S.A. New
York: Vantage Press, 1970. 156 p. Biblio.

A work of two separate and different parts. In Part I
the author, who is a New Mexican teacher, minces no
words in attempting "to explode some of the myths which
the Anglo-Saxons have invented to obscure the great
heroic achievements of other races, especially of the
Spanish." With the exception of the brief closing chapter designed to show how the oppressed have revolted
at home and abroad against Anglo-America, Part II is
the author's panoramic view of the Movimiento presented through selections taken from Chicano newspapers
such as BRONZE, EL CHICANO, EL GALLO, EL GRI-
TO, EL MALCRIADO, LA RAZA, and LA VOZ NOR-
TENA.

DA-49 Weber, David J. FOREIGNERS IN THEIR NATIVE LAND: HISTORICAL
ROOTS OF THE MEXICAN AMERICANS. Foreword by Ramon Eduardo
Ruiz. Albuquerque: University of New Mexico Press, 1973. 302 p.
Index. Notes.

An overview of Mexican American history presented
through obscure materials such as letters, memoirs, manuscripts, public records, newspaper accounts, and excerpts
from diaries, some of which have been translated for the
first time. Selections from published monographs have
also been used. Each of the five chapters is preceded
by a brief introductory statement by the editor. The
study begins with 1540 when the first explorers came to
the Southwest from Mexico, but focuses mainly on the
events of the nineteenth century. The editor establishes
that the Anglo's anti-Mexican thought and behavior--
which endures to this day--was already well founded
by 1910, the closing date of this work.

APPLIED SCIENCES

APPLIED SCIENCES

Psychology

EA-1 Wagner, Nathaniel N., and Haug, Marsha J., eds. CHICANOS: SO-
CIAL AND PSYCHOLOGICAL PERSPECTIVES. St. Louis: The C.V.
Mosby Co., 1971. 303 p. Biblio. B & w photos. Index. Refs.

> Through selected articles formerly published in profes-
> sional journals by both Chicano and non-Chicano authors,
> this book of readings presents an overview of the current
> literature which provides psychological and sociological
> outlooks on Mexican Americans. Family, personality,
> the law, education, and mental health are among the
> subjects dealt with in separate sections.

Public Health

EB-1 Clark, Margaret. HEALTH IN THE MEXICAN AMERICAN CULTURE:
A COMMUNITY STUDY. Berkeley and Los Angeles: University of Cali-
fornia Press, 1959. xii, 253 p. Biblio. Graphs. Gloss. Index.
Tables.

> Based on the author's doctoral dissertation, this work
> studies the conflict between Mexican Americans in Sal
> Si Puedes, a barrio on the eastern edge of San Jose,
> California, and the English-speaking medical personnel
> with whom they come in contact. The emphasis is on
> public health problems, but information is also presented
> on curative medicine, education, social welfare, and
> related fields. The work is intended to serve profes-
> sionals working with people of Mexican background.

EB-2 Moustafa, A. Taher, and Weiss, Gertrud. HEALTH STATUS AND PRAC-
TICES OF MEXICAN AMERICANS. Mexican American Study Project
Advance Report, no. 2. Los Angeles: Division of Research, Graduate
School of Business Administration, University of California, 1968. vii,

52 p. Biblio. Tables. Pap.

Despite the large number of Mexican Americans in the Southwest, the authors, two medical doctors, are confronted with the problem of finding differentiated health and vital statistics pertinent to the group. Significant facts in this work include the special tabulations on mortality, leading causes of death by ethnic group, prevalence of chronic conditions, and mortality rates for the State of Colorado and the City of San Antonio, to name a few.

EB-3 Saunders, Lyle. CULTURAL DIFFERENCES AND MEDICAL CARE: THE CASE OF THE SPANISH-SPEAKING PEOPLE OF THE SOUTHWEST. New York: Russell Sage Foundation, 1954. 317 p. Chap. notes. Index. Tables.

The professional credentials of the author combined with his interest in and understanding of Southwestern Mexican Americans increase the value of this work which was prepared, among other reasons, "to illustrate some of the areas and ways in which cultural factors influence the giving and accepting of medical care." The text is presented in layman's language and deals with beliefs, roles, values, attitudes, customs, etc., and how these are integrated with government, religious, family, education, and economic matters. There are more up-to-date books, but this one still merits reading. The chapter on "Healing Way" still has valid information on folk medicine and practices and further provides reasons why Anglo medicine is at times rejected by La Raza.

A PROFILE OF CHICANO
NEWSPAPERS AND PERIODICALS

A PROFILE OF CHICANO
NEWSPAPERS AND PERIODICALS

The publication explosion of recent years that has taken place in books and mono-graphs concerned with Chicanos has also extended into the realm of newspapers and periodicals. As the Chicano from the barrio finds himself more comfortable reading these types of publications, they have become particularly effective ve-hicles for carrying news about el Movimiento to the barrio. Their coverage re-flects the social unrest among Chicanos from Los Angeles on the West Coast to Chicago on the East, and from Colorado in the North to the border states of Tex-as, New Mexico, and Arizona in the South. These publications which record the pulse of Raza people in and out of the barrios and at all economic levels have generally been consolidated under the Chicano Press Association.

Not all Mexican American serial publications, however, are the result of the Chicano movement, nor are they all dedicated to la Causa. Some are conser-vative publications that usually carry noncontroversial news about La Raza, or publish what appears in establishment newspapers and magazines. Their editor-ial policy is to publish information which will appeal to the largest number of Spanish-speaking readers from all over the country and in some cases from south of the border. The language used is standard Spanish or English, or both. The target reader is obviously the middle-class Mexicanoamericano or other Latinos who can afford to subscribe to these publications.

On the other hand, there are Chicano publications which represent the liberal view. Some are more radical than others, but whether moderate or radical their objective is the same--to inform Chicanos about Chicanos on a regional ba-sis. Some of these publications dramatize issues both with words and illustra-tions. Others use a straight journalistic style of reporting the news. It is not unusual to find in these newspapers and magazines poems, corridos (ballads), and even short plays or skits written in Spanish or English or a combination of both. There are news stories that tell about police brutality, court injustices, drug ad-diction, abuse of labor rights, or simply narrate family gatherings from bautismos to velorios. The aim is to create in the Chicano an awareness of his cultural heritage and in addition to contribute useful information leading to his political and socioeconomic advancement. One of the more successful monthlies in this category is THE FORUMEER, established in 1954, which according to its editor functions as the "watchdog" for La Raza. Newspapers with a regional scope have suffered a high mortality, mostly due to the lack of dramatic issues which transcend local boundaries. EL GALLO is an example of this problem. At one time it was among the most widely read newspapers read by Chicanos in the Southwest. While it has managed to survive, it seems to have lost much of its previous prominence in the last few years.

Several student publications have surfaced as a result of the Chicano movement, usually at the college or university level. Their focus is on education issues as they affect Chicano students. The importance of the students' writings rests on the fact that they have called attention to problems which have gone unperceived or unattended to by administrators. The mortality rate of these publications is among the highest for it is not easy to carry the initial thrust of one semester over to another. So much of their success depends on individuals and the support which they can rally from their classmates.

No less important are the barrio tabloids, although some are no more than a one-page mimeographed aviso. Regardless of their formats they play an important role in providing local news in both English and Spanish to residents in Chicano neighborhoods. LA VOZ DEL BARRIO of Eagle Pass, Texas, for example, informed its readers how Model Cities funds were being spent from 1970 until June 1973. In this case, the life span of these publications often depends on the length of time there is and the need for information on specific issues. Interestingly, these neighborhood bulletins have given birth to still another type of publication--that which focuses on the concerns of the Chicana. An example is LA RAZON MESTIZA of the San Francisco Mission District. Stress is placed on information about how women must organize in order to assume more responsible roles in the Chicano movement and in society in general. Attention is also called to scholarships and employment opportunities available to women.

Los pintos also have their own publications. The scope of their writings covers the gamut. Perhaps a more accurate statement would be to say that they publish on all subjects that are not censored by institutional authorities. Their poetry, in particular, conveys to the reader a feeling of their anguish and anxieties as well as their desire to return to the barrio and join forces with other Chicanos involved in la Causa. LA PALABRA: ALAMBRE de M.A.S.H. is among pinto publications calling for justice from behind prison walls.

Since so many of the farm workers are Chicanos, it is not surprising that they should have their own publications. EL MALCRIADO and EL CAMPESINO serve as examples. Their aim is to inform farm workers and their supporters on the activities and importance of their union, the United Farm Workers of America. The bulk of the writing deals with the struggle for improved working conditions and wages. Interspersed among the writing on farm labor throughout the nation are news items on the campesino's education and cultural activities. As the farm workers are not all Chicanos, they publish in English and Spanish, and occasionally EL MALCRIADO will print news items in Ilocano and Tagalog for the benefit of its Filipino readers.

Finally, there are a few Chicano serials in the form of scholarly journals primarily concerned with publishing articles which criticize and reappraise theoretical assumptions and empirical evidence arrived at by academicians outside the Chicano group. Many of the contributors to these journals are subject specialists. Those in the humanities, literature in particular, publish in EL GRITO. AZTLAN, in turn, draws the writings of the social scientists. These two periodicals are probably the best known in their respective fields, but the product of Chicano scholars is also found in more specialized journals such as THE JOURNAL OF MEXICAN AMERICAN HISTORY and THE BILINGUAL REVIEW/LA REVISTA BILINGUE. The difficulty faced by the editors of these journals is locating sufficient and appropriate material to publish on a regular basis. The number of qualified Chicano professionals is still very limited and their writings are in great demand.

Chicano serial publications are generally not listed in standard American bibliographical sources. The 1974 AYERS DIRECTORY OF PUBLICATIONS, considered the most comprehensive directory of newspapers in the country, has a separate section for Blacks, but none for Chicanos. It does include approximately 113 titles of Spanish-language publications (newspapers and periodicals), including those from Panama, the Philippines, and Puerto Rico, all lumped together in a section entitled "Foreign Language Publications." Among these, there are possibly three titles which qualify as Chicano publications. ULRICH'S INTERNATIONAL PERIODICALS DIRECTORY, published in 1973, which includes entries for approximately 55,000 in-print periodicals published throughout the world, gives Chicano periodicals about the best coverage they have received so far, but this source is still found lacking. The highly touted ENCYCLOPEDIA DIRECTORY OF ETHNIC NEWSPAPERS IN THE UNITED STATES with its thirty-nine Spanish/English and Spanish-language newspapers bypassed Chicano publications completely.

Last March in an attempt to close this bibliographical gap, I mailed a questionnaire to 164 addressees requesting information to compile an up-to-date directory of Chicano periodicals and newspapers. The basic list of addressees was assembled by consulting various secondary sources, including Anne Jordan's "Mexican American Publishing Guide," which she compiled as part of the requirement for the Master of Arts degree at the University of Texas, Austin, and which later appeared in the first two issues of THE JOURNAL OF MEXICAN AMERICAN HISTORY published in 1973. All of the sources used had something to contribute, and in particular, that of Ms. Jordan. The problem was to decide what to select for inclusion and what to reject. The more I searched the more possible titles emerged. Often Mexican periodicals such as BOX Y LUCHA, CONFIDENCIAS, TODO, and the like appeared in Chicano bibliographies. I have excluded them. It is not unlikely that they would appeal to some Raza Spanish readers, but this still does not make them Chicano publications. Also excluded are publications known to be deceased, i.e., EL CORAJE and ALIANZA, but which continue to be cited as though currently being published in Tucson, Arizona. The directory which follows is not flawless. Already I have become aware of certain omissions. In the interest of making the necessary amendments and with the intent of compiling as comprehensive a directory as possible for a possible revised edition, I urge all users to inform me in regard to corrections or additions.

DIRECTORY OF NEWSPAPERS

AND PERIODICALS

ARRANGEMENT OF INFORMATION

Below are the items with their corresponding number and arrangement of the information provided:

1. Title (appears unnumbered in the entry)
2. Address (numbering starts with this item)
3. Date established
4. Frequency
5. Rate
6. Target reader
7. Language in which material is published
8. Name of publisher, president, or editor
9. Approximate circulation
10. Editorial orientation
11. Special features
12. If indexed, in what published source? (applies only to periodicals)

Note: A dash following a number indicates that no information was submitted or is available for this item.

SAMPLE ENTRY:

REVISTA CHICANO-RIQUENA

2. Indiana University Northwest, 3400 Broadway, Gary IN 46408.
3. Fall 1973. 4. Quarterly. 5. $5/yr. 6. Chicano and Puerto Ricans in U.S. 7. English & Spanish. 8. Nicolas Kanellos and Luis Davila, eds. 9. 500. 10. Literature and folklore. 11. Artwork, critical articles, and book reviews. 12. No.

DIRECTORY OF NEWSPAPERS
AND PERIODICALS

AHORA

2. P.O. Box 511, Alamosa, CO 81101. 3. September, 1970. 4. Monthly. 5. 10¢/copy or $4.50/yr. 6. Chicano and Mexican community. 7. English & Spanish. 8. Magdaleno Avila, LeRoy Maes, Ramon Vera, eds. 9. 4,000. 10. - . 11. Issues, events, or incidents relevant to Chicanos in Colorado (e.g., UFW strike, education, etc.).

AZTLAN: CHICANO JOURNAL OF THE SOCIAL SCIENCES & ARTS

2. Aztlan Publications, Chicano Studies Center, University of California at Los Angeles, 405 Hilgard Street, Los Angeles, CA 90024. 3. Spring 1970. 4. Semi-annual. 5. $7/yr.; libraries $10/yr.; institutions $12/yr. Rates decrease with length of subscription. 6. - . 7. English & Spanish. 8. Juan Gomez-Quinones, Reynaldo Macias, Andrew Chavez, eds. 9. 1,000. 10. Academic. 11. Special subjects are featured occasionally. 12. Yes (source not specified).

EL BAUTISTA MEXICANO

2. 305 Baptist Building, Dallas, TX 75201. 3. 1950(?). 4. Monthly. 5. $1/yr. 6. - . 7. Spanish primarily, some English. 8. Mrs. Ruby Vargas, assoc. ed. 9. 5,300. 10. None. 11. -.

THE BILINGUAL REVIEW/LA REVISTA BILINGUE

2. Department of Romance Languages, City College of New York, N.Y. 10031. 3. Spring 1974. 4. Three times per year. 5. $6/ yr.; $11/2 yrs.; $15/3 yrs. 6. International professional bilingual community and the Hispanic community of the United States. 7. English & Spanish; other dialects and languages also. 8. Gary D. Keller, ed. 9. 2,000. 10. Bilingualism. 11. Research and scholarly-oriented articles, creative literature, bibliography, reviews. Professional announcements section and books-received section. 12.

Yes. MLA INTERNATIONAL BIBLIOGRAPHY, ACTFL ANNUAL BIBLIOGRAPHY, LANGUAGE AND LANGUAGE BEHAVIOR AB-STRACTS, ABSTRACTS OF ENGLISH STUDIES.

EL CAMPESINO

2. P.O. Box 1493, San Juan, TX 78589. 3. September 1972. 4. Biweekly. 5. $4.50/yr. 6. Farm workers. 7. Spanish. 8. Alfredo de Avila. 9. 4,000. 10. Union orientation. 11. - .

CHICANO LAW REVIEW

2. University of California at Los Angeles School of Law, 405 Hilgard Avenue, Los Angeles, CA 90024. 3. Summer 1972. 4. Semiannual. 5. $12/vol. (4 issues). 6. Legal profession. 7. English. 8. David Arredondo, ed. 9. 450. 10. - . 11. - . 12. No.

EL CHICANO NEWS MAGAZINE

2. P.O. Box 827, 1265 North Mt. Vernon Avenue, Colton, CA 92324. 3. April 1969. 4. Weekly. 5. $7.50/yr.; $10/yr. institutional. 6. Mexican Americans. 7. 60-70% English; 30-40% Spanish. 8. Gloria Macias Harrison, ed. 9. 10,000. 10. Positive approach to ethnic problems. 11. - .

CHICANO TIMES

2. P.O. Box 3624, Corpus Christi, TX 78404. 3. September 1970. 4. Bimonthly. 5. - . 6. Chicano community. 7. English & Spanish. 8. Jose Luis Rodriguez, ed. and publisher; Stephen Casanova, ed., Gulf Coast. 9. 25,000. 10. Community newspaper, issues relevant to Chicanos; positive image for Chicanos; alternative press. 11. Columnist--criticism of various poverty agencies and directors.

EL DIARIO DE LA GENTE

2. U.M.C. 416, University of Colorado, Boulder, CO 80302. 3. July 1972. 4. Biweekly. 5. $5/yr. 6. Chicano students and community. 7. English primarily, & Spanish. 8. John Espinoza, Paul Mora, eds.; Leonard Maestas, summer ed. 9. 6,000. 10. Chicano. 11. - .

ECHO

2. 2801 E. 5th, Box 6354, Austin, TX 78702. 3. March 1974. 4. Biweekly. 5. $3.50/yr. 6. The Chicano. 7. English, primarily, & Spanish. 8. Zeke Romo, ed. 9. 10,000. 10. Chicano. 11. - .

THE FORUMEER

2. 127 Graham Avenue, No. 3, San Jose, CA 95110. 3. 1954.
4. Monthly. 5. - . 6. Mexican Americans. 7. English & Spanish. 8. E. David Sierra, ed. 9. 10,000 per month. 10. Encourage people to participate in political processes. 11. Articles
on Chicanos succeeding in a foreign culture; encourage Chicanismo;
be a "watch-dog" for La Raza.

LA FUERZA

2. 1811 South First Street, Austin, TX 78704. 3. March 1962.
4. Weekly. 5. $7.50/yr. mailed. 6. Mexican American. 7.
English & Spanish. 8. Jesse Garza, Jr., publisher. 9. 7,500.
10. Progressive motivational. 11. - .

EL GALLO NEWSPAPER, INC.

2. P.O. Box 18347, 1567 Downing Street, Denver, CO 80218.
3. 1967. 4. Irregular, approximately 12 issues per year. 5.
$2.50/12 issues; $7/12 issues to foreign countries. 6. Chicanos.
7. English. 8. Rodolfo "Corky" Gonzales, ed. 9. 2,000. 10.
To communicate with Chicanos in Southwest and throughout nation.
Educate on different contemporary issues that affect lives of Chicanos. 11. Highlights stories on Chicano activists. Prints Chicano
poetry; illustrates stories with photos.

LA GENTE

2. 405 Hilgard Avenue, Los Angeles, CA 90024. 3. 1970. 4.
Six times per school year. 5. $5, $7.50, $10 for 1, 5, and 10
copies respectively. 6. Those interested in Latino data. 7. English
& Spanish. 8. Jose Hernandez, ed. 9. 10,000. 10. Political,
cultural, and social. 11. None. 12. - .

GRAFICA

2. 705 North Windsor Boulevard, Hollywood, CA 90038. 3. 1947.
4. Bi-monthly. 5. $4.50/yr. 6. (see 10). 7. Spanish. 8. Ar-
mando del Moral, ed. 9. - . 10. Family oriented. 11. - .
12. - .

EL GRITO: A JOURNAL OF CONTEMPORARY MEXICAN AMERICAN THOUGHT

2. P.O. Box 9275, Berkeley, CA 94709. 3. Fall 1967. 4. Quarterly. 5. $5/yr.; $6/yr. foreign. 6. Those interested in contemporary Chicano writings. 7. English & Spanish & Chicano Spanish.
8. Octavio I. Romano-V, Ph. D. and Herminio Rios-C., eds. 9.
To provide a forum for Chicano writers and to publish the best Chi-

cano literary production in the social sciences and humanities articulating Chicano issues. 10. - . 11. Chicano artists used to illustrate stories and ideas.

EL GRITO DEL NORTE

2. Box 12547, Albuquerque, NM 87105. 3. August 1968. 4. Biweekly at first; later monthly; suspended in August 1973; now publishing a 4-page newsletter. 5. - . 6. Poor and working class raza. 7. English & Spanish. 8. Betita Martinez, ed. 9. 10,000. 10. Revolutionary nationalism. 11. Some features on issues in Mexico, Latin America, and other Third World struggles.

LA GUARDIA LTD.

2. 805 South 5th Street, Room 306, Milwaukee WI 53204. 3. August 1969. 4. Monthly. 5. Free. 6. Mexican and Puerto Rican communities. 7. English & Spanish. 8. Ricardo Villareal, ed.; Esteban Martinez, asst. ed. and photographer. 9. 6,000. 10. Varies. 11. Publishes a calendar.

EL HISPANO

2. P.O. Box 2201, 900 Silver Avenue, S.W., Albuquerque, NM 87102. 3. June 1966. 4. Weekly. 5. $4/yr.; $4.50/yr. outside NM. 6. Spanish-speaking people. 7. Spanish. 8. Angel B. Collado, publisher and ed. 9. 8,000. 10. Educational and cultural. 11. -.

IDEAL

2. P.O. Box 21, Coachella, CA 92201. 3. September 1969. 4. Semi-monthly. 5. $5/yr. 6. Mexican American. 7. English & Spanish. 8. Al Fuller, Ray Rodriguez, eds. 9. 6,000 per issue. 10. - . 11. - .

EL INDEPENDIENTE & THE NEW MEXICO INDEPENDENT

2. P.O. Box 429, Albuquerque, NM 87103. 3. 1896. 4. Weekly. 5. $5/yr. 6. High school level and up. 7. English & Spanish. 8. Mark D. Acuff, ed. 9. 9,500 (4 editions). 10. Politics, arts, and media. 11. New Mexico's only source of media criticism.

EL INFORMADOR

2. 1510 West 18th Street, Chicago, IL 60608. 3. February 1964. 4. Weekly. 5. - . 6. El Mexicano. 7. 98% Spanish, 2% English. 8. - . 9. 20,000. 10. - . 11. Listing of theaters in Chicago showing films in Spanish.

THE JOURNAL OF MEXICAN AMERICAN HISTORY

2. P.O. Box 13861, University of California at Santa Barbara, Santa Barbara, CA 93107. 3. Fall 1970. 4. Annually; two issues in one publication published in December of year. 5. $10. 6. Scholars interested in Mexican American history. 7. English. 8. Ruben Cortez, publisher; Joseph Navarro, ed.; Allan Figueroa Deck, Ph.D., assoc. ed. 9. Throughout 50 states in universities, colleges, and public libraries. 10. - . 11. Historical research. 12. Yes. HISTORICAL ABSTRACTS and/or AMERICA: HISTORY AND LIFE.

THE LAREDO TIMES

2. P.O. Box 29, Laredo, TX 78040. 3. Early 1800s. 4. Daily. 5. - . 6. Community newspaper. 7. English & Spanish. 8. Fernando Pinon, managing ed. 9. 20,000. 10. Moderate-liberal. 11. - .

LA LUZ

2. 360 South Monroe, Suite 320, Denver, CO 80209. 3. March 1972. 4. Monthly. 5. $7.50/yr.; $13.50/2 yrs. 6. Educated middle class. 7. English. 8. Daniel Velez, publisher; Dr. Philip D. Ortego, ed.-in-chief. 9. 35,000. 10. To present all facets of the life style of the Spanish-speaking people in the United States. Desires to contribute to spiritual, economic, political, social, and moral betterment of Spanish-speaking people. 11. Abundant photos. Includes literature--poetry, drama, etc., and brief reviews of recently published books. 12. No.

EL MALCRIADO

2. P.O. Box 62, Keene, CA 93531. 3. 1962. 4. Every three or four weeks. 5. 10¢/copy or $5/bundle of 50. 6. Farm workers and farm worker supporters. 7. English & Spanish. 8. Venustiano Olguin, Jr., ed.; Nancy Destefanis, business manager. 9. 35,000. 10. Official voice of the United Farm Workers of America recording the struggle of farm workers for their union. 11. Has published some items in the four major languages of the membership: English, Spanish, Ilocano, and Tagalog.

MANO A MANO

2. 3520 Montrose, Suite 216, Houston, TX 77006. 3. - . 4. Bi-monthly. 5. $4/yr. 6. Those interested in delivery of social services and mental health services to Chicanos. 7. English. 8. Elena R. Gonzalez, ed. 9. 300. 10. Social services and mental health services to Chicanos and all related social issues. 11. - .

EL MESTIZO

2. M.E. Ch. A., Box 160, University of Texas at El Paso, El Paso, TX 79968. 3. December 1973. 4. Bimonthly. 5. $2.50/yr. 6. - . 7. English & Spanish. 8. - . 9. 2,500. 10. - . 11. - . 12. No.

EL MUNDO

2. 630 - 20th Street, Oakland, CA 94612. 3. 1966. 4. Weekly. 5. - . 6. San Francisco Bay Latinos. 7. English & Spanish. 8. Thomas Berkeley, publisher; Abdon J. Ugarte, ed. 9. 25,000. 10. Latin people. 11. - .

NCHO NEWSLETTER: "SALUD Y REVOLUCION SOCIAL"

2. 1709 W. 8th Street, Suite 517, Los Angeles, CA 90017. 3. July 1971. 4. Monthly. 5. None. 6. Health care professionals, college, university, and high school students, community-at-large. 7. English. 8. Pete Romo, ed. 9. 10,000. 10. To provide information on health to the Spanish-speaking people on a national basis with regional emphasis on the Southwest and Midwest. 11. Health news; information on health as it pertains to students; some information on cultural awareness.

NEW MEXICO INDEPENDENT

(see EL INDEPENDIENTE)

NOSOTROS MAGAZINE

2. 812 North Virginia Street, El Paso, TX 79902. 3. January 1971. 4. Monthly. 5. 25¢/copy. 6. High school and college student. 7. English and Spanish. 8. Arturo Franco, ed. 9. 5,000. 10. - . 11. Editorial page. 12. No.

LA OPINION: DIARIO POPULAR INDEPENDIENTE

2. 1436 South Main Street, Los Angeles, CA 90015. 3. September 1926. 4. Daily. 5. 10¢/copy. 6. Spanish-speaking from Mexico and Latin America. 7. Spanish. 8. Ignacio E. Lozano, Sr., founder; Ignacio E. Lozano, Jr., present director; Alfredo Gonzales, publisher. 9. 25,000. 10. Focuses on news and information of particular interest to Mexicans and Mexican Americans in the Los Angeles area. Orientation is generally conservative. 11. Special feature stories on topics with appeal for first and second generation Mexican Americans and new Americans from other Latin American countries.

LA PALABRA: ALAMBRE DE M.A.S.H.

2. M.A.S.H., Box 500, Steilacoom, WA 98388. 3. March 1969.
4. Quarterly. 5. None. 6. Members and supporters of Mexican
American Self Help (M.A.S.H.) and concerned people. 7. English
& Spanish. 8. - . 9. 600. 10. One of the few newspapers of
its kind in that it endeavors to disseminate information of special
interest to Chicano prison inmates. 11. Articles concerned with
La Causa and its related Movimiento.

PRENSA POPULAR

2. Rosaura Sanchez, c/o Third World Studies, University of California at San Diego, San Diego, CA 92307. 3. September 1973.
4. Monthly. 5. $5/yr. 6. Chicano community. 7. English &
Spanish. 8. - . 9. 7,000. 10. Marxist-Leninist (Socialist). 11.
Special emphasis on struggles of Chicanos, Latin America, working
class, and women.

RASSA LOBBYIST

2. 400 First Street, N.W., Suite 706, Washington, D.C. 20001.
3. May 1973. 4. Monthly. 5. $50/yr. subscription-membership.
6. Spanish-speaking and general public. 7. English. 8. Manuel
D. Fierro, ed. 9. 10,000. 10. Legislative issues affecting Spanish-speaking peoples. 11. Highlights congressional activities of
Congressmen and Senators.

LA RAZA MAGAZINE

In late 1960s LA RAZA NEWSPAPER merged with CHICANO STU-
DENT MOVEMENT NEWSPAPER to create the present magazine.
2. P.O. Box 31004, Los Angeles, CA 90031. 3. 1967 (tabloid),
1970 (periodical). 4. Monthly. 5. $10/yr. 6. Chicano communi-
ty. 7. Spanish & English. 8. - . 9. 10,000. 10. Serves as or-
gan of the Movimiento; aims for equality, justice, and an end to
discrimination. 11. Reflects events and life in the barrios. Includes reader's letters, editorials, articles centered on Chicano culture and social commentary on farm workers' activities, prison news,
and educational abuses. 12. - .

LA RAZON MESTIZA

2. 2588 Mission Street, Room 201, San Francisco, CA 94110. 3.
March 1974. Monthly. 5. $2/yr. 6. Chicanas; ethnic and wo-
men's studies. 7. English & Spanish. 8. Dorinda Moreno, ed.
9. 1,000. 10. Chicana education and activism. 11. Listings of
available scholarships and job openings for Chicanas.

EL RENACIMIENTO

2. 915 North Washington, Lansing, MI 48906. 3. March 1970.
4. Semi-monthly. 5. $3 minimum donation. 6. Spanish-speaking.
7. English & Spanish. 8. Edmundo Georgi, ed. and dir. 9.
10,000. 10. Emphasis on the achievement of Raza self-determina-
tion. 11. - .

REVISTA CHICANO-RIQUENA

2. Indiana University Northwest, 3400 Broadway, Gary, IN 46408.
3. Fall 1973. 4. Quarterly. 5. $5/yr. 6. Chicano and Puerto
Ricans in U.S. 7. English & Spanish. 8. Nicolas Kanellos and
Luis Davila, eds. 9. 500. 10. Literature and folklore. 11. Art-
work, critical articles, and book reviews. 12. No.

EL SOL DE TEXAS

2. 1802 Spann Avenue, Dallas, TX 75207. 3. September 30,
1966. 4. Weekly. 5. $9/yr. 6. Spanish-speaking population in
the Southwest. 7. Eighty percent Spanish and twenty percent English. 8. Jesus Gutierrez E., owner. 9. 100,000. 10. Independent. 11. Photo resume of weekly events.

EL TECOLOTE

2. 1292 Potrero, San Francisco, CA 94110. 3. August 1970. 4.
Currently monthly, semi-monthly in near future. 5. $5/yr. 6.
Raza communities; young and old. 7. English & Spanish. 8. Juan
Gonzales, publisher. 9. 5,000. 10. Crusade for political aware-
ness and general information within community. 11. Section on
art, activities in Latin America, noticias section. Interviews with
Raza personalities.

LA VERDAD

2. P.O. Box 70, 123 West Edwards Street, Cristal City, TX 78839.
3. 1970. 4. Bi-weekly. 5. 25¢/ copy. 6. Mexican American
community of Texas in particular. 7. English & Spanish. 8. Luz
Gutierrez, Rafael Torres, and Carolina Tovar, eds. 9. 4,000.
10. To provide communication among Mexican Americans, locally,
and throughout the Southwest, and to serve as a vehicle for the
Chicano movement. 11. - .

LA VOZ

2. P.O. Box 19206, Diamond Lake Station, Minneapolis, MN
55419. 3. 1970. 4. Monthly. 5. $3/yr. 6. Chicano and An-
glo community, locally and nationwide. 7. English & spanish.

8. David J. Ramirez, ed. and founder. 9. Distributed in 22 states and parts of Mexico. 10. Chicano issues. 11. Local Chicano social events, articles on local personalities.

LA VOZ DEL PUEBLO

2. 2732 Durant Avenue, Berkeley, CA 94704. 3. June 1970. 4. Monthly. 5. $3.50/yr. 6. Chicanos of Bay Area. 7. English & Spanish. 8. Frente Foundation, Inc., publisher; Agustin Gurza, ed. 9. 6,000. 10. Left of center. 11. Character feature stories. 12. - .

Listed below are titles and addresses of periodicals and newspapers from which no reply was received. An asterisk preceeding a title indicates that the questionnaire was returned by the post office because the addressee could not be located at the address cited or because no forwarding address was designated. Unmarked titles simply show that the questionnaire was not returned.

EL AGUILA. 2028 City View Avenue, Los Angeles, CA 90033.

EL ALACRAN-MECHA. California State College, Long Beach, CA 90804.

EL ALAMBRE DE MAYO. c/o MAYO Sponsor, Box 535, Corona, CA 91720.

ALAMO MESSENGER. 207 Arden Grove, San Antonio, TX.

AMERICA and AMERICA HISPANA. 2448 Mission Street, San Francisco, CA 94110.

ATISBOS. P.O. Box 2362, Stanford University, Stanford, CA 94305.

BASTA YA! Box 40040, San Francisco, CA 94110.

BRONZE. 142 Pickford Avenue, San Jose, CA 95127.

CARTA EDITORIAL. P.O. Box 54624, Terminal Annex, Los Angeles, CA 90054.

*LA CAUSA. 5116 E. Whittier Boulevard, Los Angeles, CA 90054.

CHICANA. Chino Institute for Women, P.O. Box 800, Ontario, CA 91761.

CHICANISMO. 560 Alvarado Row, Stanford, CA 94305.

*EL CHICANO. Box 1416, Fort Worth, TX 76101.

*EL CHICANO. 4021 First Avenue, San Bernardino, CA 92410.

CHICANO COMMUNITY NEWSPAPER. 1265 North Mt. Vernon Avenue, Colton, CA 92324.

CHICANO RESEARCH: THE JOURNAL OF THE MEXICAN AMERICAN EDUCATION PROJECT. 600 Jay Street, SCI-317, Sacramento, CA 95819.

CHICANO STUDENT MOVEMENT. Box 31322, Los Angeles, CA 90031.

CHICANO TIMES. 719 Delgado, San Antonio, TX 78207.

*CHICANO TIMES. 719 Delgade, San Francisco, CA 94118.

EL CHISME. Sid Richardson Hall 1326, University of Texas, Austin, TX 78712.

LA CHISPA. Chicano Studies Center, 5716 Lindo Paseo, San Diego, CA.

COLUMNAS. 418 Main Street, Davenport, IA 52801.

*COMMUNITY UNITED FRONT: PEOPLE'S NEWS SERVICE. 4701 East 12th Street, Austin, TX.

COMPASS, 1209 Egypt Street, Houston, TX 77009.

*CON SAFOS: REFLECTIONS OF LIFE IN THE BARRIO. P.O. Box 31004, Los Angeles, CA 90031.

EL CONTINENTAL. 218 S. Campbell Street, Box 1950, El Paso, TX 79901. Also, 909 E. San Antonio Street, El Paso, TX 79902.

EL CUADERNO: ACADEMIA DE LA NUEVA RAZA. c/o Tomas Atencio, P.O. Box 148, Dixon, NM 87527.

CUERVE INTERNATIONAL: VANGUARD POETRY REVIEW. P.O. Box 17645, Hollywood, CA.

*EL DEGUELLO. Box 37094, San Antonio, TX 78237.

EL DESPERTADOR DE TEJAS. University of Texas, Austin, TX.

EASTSIDE SUN/MEXICAN AMERICAN SUN. 319 North Soto Street, San Jose, CA.

EDITORIAL. P.O. Box 1881, El Paso, TX.

ENTRELINEAS. Penn Valley Community College Services, 560 Westport Road, Kansas City, MO 64111.

ES TIEMPO. MECHA, Foothill College, 12345 El Monte Avenue, Los Altos Hills, CA 94022.

EL EXCENTRICO MAGAZINE. 195 Devine Street, San Jose, CA.

EL EXITO. P.O. Box 229, Beeville, TX 78102.

FLATBOTTOM NEWS. 1103 East North Street, Victoria, TX 77901.

EL FRONTERIZO. 909 East San Antonio Street, El Paso, TX 79901.

LA GENTE DE AZTLAN. 308 Westwood Plaza, Los Angeles, CA 90024.

EL GOLPE AVISA. Box 2321, Waco, TX.

HASTA (Hispanic Americans Striving Toward Advancement). 4000 Cooper Street, Jackson, MI 49201.

EL HERALDO DE BROWNSVILLE. Freedom Newspapers, Inc., P.O. Box 351, Brownsville, TX.

EL HISPANO. P.O. Box 2853, Sacramento, CA 95818.

EL HISPANO-AMERICANO. 630 Ninth Street, Sacramento, CA 95825.

HOY. Cabinet Committee on Opportunity for Spanish-speaking Peoples, 1707 H Street, N.W., Washington, DC 20506.

INDEPENDENT OF VALENCIA COUNTY. P.O. Box 429, Albuquerque, NM 87101.

EL INDEPENDIENTE OF SANTA FE COUNTY. P.O. BOX 429, Albuquerque, NM 87101.

*INFERNO. 321 Frio City Road, San Antonio, TX 78207.

*INSIDE EASTSIDE. P.O. Box 63273, Los Angeles, CA 90063.

*EL INSURGENTE. General Delivery, Laredo, TX 78040.

*JOURNAL OF MEXICAN AMERICAN STUDIES. Mexican American Documentation and Educational Research Institute, 1229 East Cypress Street, Anaheim, CA 92805.

*LADO. 1306 North Western Avenue, Chicago, IL 60622.

LAMA Newsletter. 1728 East Fourteenth Street, San Leandro, CA 94577.

LAND OF TWO. P.O. Box 409, Davis, CA 95616.

LULAC Newsletter. 2590 Morgan Street, Corpus Christi, TX.

EL MACHETE. MECHA, Los Angeles City College, 855 North Vermont Avenue, Los Angeles, CA 90026.

*MAGAZIN (formerly CHICANO TIMES MAGAZINE). P.O. Box 37345, San Antonio, TX 78237. Also, 417 West Craig, San Antonio, TX 78212.

MECHA Newsletter. 5151 State College Drive, Los Angeles, CA 90024.

EL MEXICANO. 909 East San Antonio Street, El Paso, TX 79901.

THE MILITANT. 14 Charles Lane, New York, NY 10014.

MIQUIZTLI. Stanford University, Building 1, Room 1B, Stanford, CA 94305.

EL MONITOR: ORGANO INFORMATIVO MENSUAL. P.O. Box 28403, San Antonio, TX 78228.

LOS MUERTOS HABLAN. 1903 Bruni, Laredo, TX 78040. Also, P.O. Box 2389, Corpus, Christi, TX.

EL MUNDO. P.O. Box 489, Berkeley, CA 94701.

NOTAS DE KINGSVILLE. 520 North Seventh Street, Kingsville, TX.

EL NOTICERO. Empleo por Unidad, Inc., P.O. Box 2000, Vacaville, CA 95688.

NUESTRAS PALABRAS. 6310 Empire Way South, Seattle, WA 98118.

EL NUEVO MEXICANO. P.O. Box 2048, Santa Fe, NM 87501.

EL OJO. 1700 K Street, N.W., Suite 1207, Washington, DC 20006.

OPEN FORUM. 323 West Fifth Street, Los Angeles, CA 90013.

LA OTRA VOZ. 102 North Guadalupe, San Marcos, TX.

EL PAISANO. P.O. Box 155, Tolleson, AZ 85353.

*LA PALABRA. P.O. Box 4879, Station C, San Jose, CA 95114.

EL PAPEL. Box 7167, Albuquerque, NM 87104.

*PAPEL CHICANO. 5141 Clay, Houston, TX 77023.

PEOPLE'S WORLD. 1819 Tenth Street, Berkeley, CA 94710.

*EL POCHO CHE. P.O. Box 4426, Berkeley, CA 94704. Also 5817 Dover Street, Oakland, CA 94609.

*EL POPO MECHA. Box 1876, Pacoima, CA 91331.

*POR MIENTRAS. P.O. Box 12761, Austin, TX 78711.

EL PORTAVOZ. P.O. Box 37365, San Antonio, TX 78237.

POST/EL MUNDO HISPANO. 2973 Sacramento Street, Berkeley, CA 94702.

LA PRENSA. 2973 Sacramento Street, Berkeley, CA 94702.

EL PUERTO DE BROWNSVILLE. 505 E. Jackson Street (Box 2054), Brownsville, TX.

*QUETZAL: JOURNAL OF NATIVE AMERICA, LA RAZA COSMICA. P.O. Box 696, Pembroke, NC 28372.

LA RAZA. P.O. Box 31004, Los Angeles, CA 90031.

LA RAZA DE BRONCE. Youth Training School, P.O. Box 800, Ontario, CA 91761.

*LA RAZA NUEVA. 2815 West Commerce, San Antonio, TX 78207.

*LA RAZA UNIDA NEWSLETTER. 6100 Dorothy, Detroit, MI 48211.

*EL REBOZO. P.O. Box 3707, San Antonio, TX.

REGENERACION (supersedes CARTA EDITORIAL). P.O. Box 54624, Terminal Annex, Los Angeles, CA 90054.

*EL RELAMPAGO. P.O. Box 128, Woodburn, OR 97071.

*LA REVOLUCION. Box 1852, Uvalde, TX 78801.

RIO GRANDE HERALD. P.O. Box 491, 201 East Main Street, Rio Grande City, TX 78582.

*SAL SI PUEDES. Community Service Center, 423 N. Milpas Street, Santa Barbara, CA 93103.

SANDOVAL COUNTY TIMES-IMMIGRANT. P.O. Box 429, Albuquerque, NM 87101

EL SOL. P.O. Box 1448, Phoenix, Arizona 85001.

SPACE CITY. 1217 Wichita, Houston, TX 77001.

STREET JOURNAL. P.O. Box 1332, San Diego, CA 92112.

SUN. P.O. Box 2171, San Antonio, TX 78297.

EL TACATE. La Raza Studies, California State University, San Francisco, CA.

TEATROS NATIONAL DE AZTLAN. P.O. Box 8096, San Diego, CA.

*EL TENAZ. P.O. Box 2302, Fresno, CA 93702.

VALLEY OF THE DAMNED. 2020 Santa Rita Avenue, Laredo, TX 78040.

VALLEY OF THE DAMNED. P.O. Box 2389, Corpus Christi, TX.

*LA VERDAD. P.O. Box 13156, San Diego, CA 92113.

LA VERDAD. 910 Francisca Street, Corpus Christi, TX 78405.

LA VIDA NUEVA. 5357 East Brooklyn Avenue, East Los Angeles College, Los Angeles, CA 90022.

VOICE OF THE CITY. 501 West Euclid, Phoenix, AZ 85041.

LA VOZ. 929 North Bonnie Beach Place, Los Angeles, CA 90063.

LA VOZ CHICANA. P.O. Box 907, San Juan, TX 78589.

LA VOZ DE AZTLAN. P.O. Box 315, St. Mary's College, CA 94575.

LA VOZ DE LA ALIANZA. 1010 Third Street, NW, Albuquerque, NM 87101.

LA VOZ DE LOS LLANOS. 1007A Avenue G, Lubbock TX 79401.

LA VOZ DEL BARRIO. P.O. Box 1632, Eagle Pass, TX 78852. (Note: Ceased publication as of June 30, 1973.)

LA VOZ DEL CHICANO. Box 2530 North, Soledad, CA 93960.

LA VOZ DEL PUEBLO. Centro Calitlan. P.O. Box 737, Hayward, CA 94543.

YA MERO! P.O. Box 1044, McAllen, TX 78501.

*EL YAQUI-COMPASS, Box 8706, Houston, TX 77009.

DIRECTORY OF PUBLISHERS

DIRECTORY OF PUBLISHERS

La Academia de la Nueva Raza
P.O. Box 148
Dixon, NM 87527

Amarex Press
Chicano Research Institute
P.O. Box 12403
El Paso, TX 79923

Ancient City Press
P.O. Box 5401
Santa Fe, NM 87501

Association of Mexican American
    Educators, Inc.
University of California
Davis, CA 95616

Aztlan Publications
Chicano Studies Center
University of California
405 Hilgard Avenue
Los Angeles, CA 90031

Barrio Publications
P.O. Box 88
Denver, CO 80201

El Barrio Publications Project
P.O. Box 31004
Los Angeles, CA 90031

Biblioteca Campesina
Stanislaus County Free Library
1402 Eye Street
Modesto, CA 95354

La Causa Publications
P.O. Box 4818
Santa Barbara, CA 93103

Centro de Estudios Chicanos
University of Washington
Seattle, WA 98105

Centro de Estudios Chicanos
    Publications
P.O. Box 4409
San Diego, CA 92104

Comite de Mexico y Aztlan
P.O. Box 12062
Oakland, CA 94604

Cucaracha Publications
El Centro Campesino Cultural
P.O. Box 1274
San Juan Bautista, CA 95045

Ediciones Pocho-Che
P.O. Box 1959
San Francisco, CA 94101

Editorial Peregrinos
2740 Aurora Drive
Tucson, AZ 85706

Educational Consortium of America
P.O. Box 1057
Menlo Park, CA 94025

Farmworker Press, Inc.
P.O. Box 62
Keene, CA 93531

Hammer Press
Relevant Instructional Materials
P.O. Box 794
Stockton, CA 95201

El Jalamate
El Centro de Informacion de la Raza
3174 24th Street
San Francisco, CA 94110

Library Development Program
Organization of American States
Washington, DC 20006

Materiales en Marcha
2950 National Avenue
San Diego, CA 92113

Mexican American Documentation &
    Educational Research Institute
1229 East Cypress Street
Anaheim, CA 92805

Migrant Referral Project
1501 Guadalupe
Austin, TX 78701

Monta Education Associates
1700 K Street, NW, Suite 1207
Washington, DC 20006

National Concilio for Chicano Studies
1700 K Street, NW, Suite 1207
Washington, DC 20006

Nunca Jamas Press
919 North Columbia Avenue
Claremont, CA 91711

Orbe Publications, Inc.
705 North Windsor Boulevard
Hollywood, CA 90038

Origenes Publications
La Raza Studies
Fresno State College
Fresno, CA

Patty-Lar Publications Ltd.
P.O. Box 4177
Mountain View, CA 94040

Perspective Publications
P.O. Box 3563
La Puente, CA

Quinto Sol Publications
P.O. Box 9275
Berkeley, CA 94709

R and E Research Associates
4843 Mission Street
San Francisco, CA 94112

La Raza Associates
2633 Granite Avenue, NW
Albuquerque, NM

Rio Grande Press, Inc.
La Casa Escuela
Glorieta, NM 87535

San Marcos Press
Box 53
Cerrillos, NM 87010

Southwest Network
1020 B Street
Hayward, CA

Tate Gallery
P.O. Box 428
Truchas, NM 87578

El Teatro de la Esperanza, Inc.
P.O. Box 1082
Goleta, CA 93017

Tlaquilo Publications
P.O. Box 7217
Los Angeles, CA 90022

Truchas Publications, Inc.
P.O. Box 5223
Lubbock, TX 79417

El Valle Publications
3946 Federal Boulevard
Denver, CO 80211

Ventura Press
P.O. Box 2268
Sunnyvale, CA

GLOSSARY

GLOSSARY

Aficionado. Enthusiast.

Alabado. Religious hymn.

Alabanza. Religious hymn.

Angelito. Painted or carved representation of a spiritual being.

Baisa. "Hand" in Chicano Spanish argot.

Barrio. Chicano neighborhood.

Bautismo. Social gathering to celebrate a christening.

Bote. "Jail" in Chicano Spanish argot.

Bracero. Mexican farm worker.

Bruja. Witch.

Bulto. Carved or sculptured representation of a saint or religious personage.

Calo. Jargon of the Spanish gypsies. By extension the Chicano Spanish argot.

Campesino. Field worker.

Cancion. For the most part a lyrical folk song with no definite verse form. Themes cover a wide range of subjects.

Causa, la. Rallying principle which unites Chicanos struggling to improve their political and socioeconomic status.

Chicanismo. Unifying philosophy which has emerged with the Chicano Movement.

Chicanito. Chicano child. Diminuitive of Chicano.

Glossary

Conquistadores. Spanish conquerors of Mexico and Peru in the sixteenth century.

Corrido. Narrative folk ballad with a uniform metrical structure of eight syllable verses. Its themes are usually limited to the tragic or heroic, or special events.

Cuando. Ballad-type song whose verses frequently being with cuando, thus the origin of the name. Narrative is usually satirical.

Curandero, -a. Healer. Medicine man or woman.

Decima. Folk song of Spanish origin that dates back to the fifteenth century. Originally it was limited to the ten line stanza. The themes cover various human experiences--from religious to the obscene.

Gabacho. Term used to designate an Anglo American.

Gente de razon. Well-to-do Hispanos.

Gorras Blancas. Secret organization in New Mexico which fought Anglo American invaders.

Hechiceria. Sorcery.

Hierbas. Herbes.

Hispano. Spanish-speaking of New Mexico.

Huelga. Strike.

Indita. Dance-song or folk dance.

Jura. "Policeman" in Chicano Spanish argot.

La Causa. See Causa, la.

La Raza. See Raza, la.

La Raza Unida. See Raza Unida, la.

Latinos. Broad term used to designate Americans of Hispanic heritage.

Maestro. Master.

Mestizo. Person of mixed Spanish and Amerindian blood.

Mexicano. Common term used by Mexican Americans to identify themselves. The Spanish word does not have the stigma of the English word.

Movimiento. Chicano civil rights movement.

Mujer mexicana. Mexican woman.

Norteno. Term used by Mexicans to designate those who seasonally cross the border, not always legally, to work for the purpose of acquiring American dollars.

Pachuquismos. Terms of Chicano Spanish argot.

Penitente. A flagellant brother of the New Mexico religious order whose origin is traced to the Third Order of St. Francis.

Pinto. Prison inmate.

Pocho. Terms used by Mexicans to designate Mexican Americans.

Politico. Politician.

Porfiriato. The years of the Porfirio Diaz regime.

Raza, La. Popular, self-applied term often used to designate Mexican Americans as a group.

Raza Unida, La. Name of the Chicano political party.

Retablo. Religious painting.

Romance. Traditional ballads. Most date back to sixteenth century or earlier Spain and a few to colonial Mexico and New Mexico.

Santo. Saint and by extension the carved or painted representations of saints and religious personages.

Tecato. Drug addict.

Tejano. Texan.

Vaquero. Western horseman.

INDEXES

AUTHOR INDEX

Author Index

TITLE INDEX OF MONOGRAPHS
AND PERIODICALS

A

ACROSS THE TRACKS: MEXICAN AMERICANS IN A TEXAS CITY 75

AFRO- AND MEXICAN-AMERI-CANA: BOOKS AND MATERI-LS IN THE LIBRARY OF FRESNO STATE COLLEGE RELATING TO THE HISTORY, CULTURE AND PROBLEMS OF AFRO- AND MEXICAN AMERICANS 6

EL AGUILA 147

AHORA 139

EL ALACRAN-MECHA 147

ALAMBRE DE M.A.S.H. 132

EL ALAMBRE DE MAYO 147

ALAMO MESSENGER 147

AL CIELO SE SUBE A PIE 38

ALIANZA 133

AMERICA 147

AMERICA HISPANA 147

AMERICAN ME 33

AMERICAN-MEXICAN FRONTIER: NUECES COUNTY, TEXAS, AN 94

AMONG THE VALIANT: MEXICAN AMERICANS IN WW II AND KOREA 16

ANDO SANGRANDO (I AM BLEED-ING): A STUDY OF MEXICAN AMERICAN-POLICE CONFLICT 99

ANNOTATED BIBLIOGRAPHY OF MATERIALS ON THE MEXICAN AMERICAN 47

ANNOTATED BIBLIOGRAPHY OF SPANISH FOLKLORE IN NEW MEXICO AND SOUTHERN COLO-RADO, AN 79

ANNUAL REPORT, FISCAL YEAR 1971 101

ANTOLOGIA DEL SABER POPULAR: A SELECTION FROM VARIOUS GENRES OF MEXICAN FOLKLORE ACROSS BORDERS 82

N